God Gardened East

God Gardened EAST

A Gardener's Meditation on the Dynamics of Genesis

LOUIS A. RUPRECHT JR.

CASCADE *Books* • Eugene, Oregon

GOD GARDENED EAST
A Gardener's Meditation on the Dynamics of Genesis

Copyright © 2008 Louis A. Ruprecht Jr. All rights reserved. Except for brief quotations in critical publications or reviews, no part of this book may be reproduced in any manner without prior written permission from the publisher. Write: Permissions, Wipf & Stock, 199 W. 8th Ave., Eugene, OR 97401.

Cascade Books
A Division of Wipf and Stock Publishers
199 W. 8th Ave., Suite 3
Eugene, OR 97401

New Revised Standard Version Bible, copyright 1989, Division of Christian Education of the National Council of the Churches of Christ in the United States of America. Used by permission. All rights reserved.

ISBN 13: 978-1-55635-434-2

Cataloging-in-Publication data:

Ruprecht, Louis A., Jr.

God gardened east : a gardener's meditation on the dynamics of Genesis / Louis A. Ruprecht Jr.

    xii + 172 p.; 23 cm.

    ISBN 13: 978-1-55635-434-2

    1. Bible. O.T. Genesis—Criticism, interpretation, etc. 2. Gardening—Philosophy. I. Title

BS1235.53 R86 2008

Manufactured in the U.S.A.

This book grew out of an earlier essay, "God Gardened in the East, Avram Wandered West." *South Atlantic Quarterly* 98.4 (1999) 689–710, used with the permission of the editor of *South Atlantic Quarterly*. Images of James Ussher and Novatus Lee Barker's 1917 graduation photograph used with the permission of Emory University's Special Collections. Images of Novatus Lee Barker's house and dry goods store used with permission of the Chattahoochee Society of West Point, Georgia, and Cobb Memorial Archives in Valley, Alabama. Images of Barker's hitching stone and the author's grandfather used with the permission of Our Labor of Love, Inc. (www.OurLaborOfLove.com). Image of the author's garden and workspace used with the permission of Louis A. Ruprecht Jr.

Quotations from the Qur'an are taken from *The Koran with a Parallel Arabic Text*, trans. N. J. Dawood (New York: Penguin Books, 1995), and *The Essential Koran*, trans. Thomas Cleary (San Francisco: HarperSanFrancisco, 1993).

This book is dedicated to my sacred circle—to Jim and Eve, to Melanie, to Larry and Barb, to Tim and Mary—and to the next generation—to Sophie and Adrian, Emma and Sarah, Michael and Oscar.

With warmest love.

Farming in this world requires the cooperation of four essential elements. . . . Faith is the earth, in which we take root; hope is the water through which we are nourished; love is the air through which we grow; knowledge is the light in which we ripen.

—The Gospel of Philip, ¶79 (third century CE)

Table of Contents

Acknowledgments ix

Preliminaries: Counting Costs 1

one Soil 19

two Sun (Genesis 1:1—2:4) 26

three East (2:4–25) 42

four Labor (3:1—4:26) 55

five Water (5:1—9:29) 69

six Grafting (10:1—12:3) 81

seven Fire (12:4—19:38) 91

eight Land (17:1—23:20) 101

nine Generation (24:1—25:11) 118

ten Sleep (24:2—50:26) 129

eleven Waking 147

Appendix: First Law, Second Law, Divine Law 163

Bibliography 167

Acknowledgments

Some books grow slowly. In this case, germination has taken a decade. In such a time, one accumulates large debts, the scale of which far surpasses one's ability to say, or repay. How, after all, can we ever adequately express our gratitude to a garden—other than to savor it, to revel in its largesse, to tend it with care? And, perhaps, to offer a gentle word of thanks. There is a lesson about piety in this, I think. And loving attention. And mortality as well. I will speak often of such things.

My adjacent landlords, Ginger Lyon, and Susanna Chavez, have ever been generous and forgiving patrons as well as genuine partners on the property we inhabit. I am grateful to them both for making me feel so very much at home in theirs. I am still more grateful to Whitney and Jesse Chamberlin, and to their son Gracyn, for being the sort of neighbors one dreams about but rarely ever gets to know. They are responsible for several of the images in this volume, for which I am deeply appreciative.

Candace Ward of South Atlantic Quarterly first put me in touch with Australian scholar Peter Murphy, who in turn put me in touch with his friend Michael Crozier, who then just so happened to be guest-editor in charge of a marvelous SAQ volume on "Gardens and Landscapes." Their kind invitation to contribute an essay to that volume in 1997 first put me onto these ideas, though as I now see it, they merely planted the seed.

As I try to explain in the introduction, the whole shape and texture of this book was changed after September 11, 2001. A bad storm or a hard freeze can literally kill a garden, forcing one to pick up, dust off, and start over. This I tried to do, and the book's form now is in large measure a result of that painstaking re-landscaping. Along the way, when I was not in my garden but working elsewhere, I have been richly blessed with students and colleagues—at Emory University, Barnard College, Princeton University, Duke University, Mercer University, the Claremont School of Theology and Graduate University, and now Georgia State University—many of whom have left their lasting imprint on words and thoughts that are mine only in the loosest sense. Gardens belong to no one; you learn that pretty quickly in the vast adventure of it all.

One of the very finest of my students, Charlie Collier, came back into my life after a happenstance meeting one year ago. I am both moved and grateful to acknowledge him as my editor at Wipf and Stock Publishers, one who has made some very important and very delicate improvements to this manuscript by urging further weeding and replanting. It is a supreme joy when students become colleagues, then friends.

Other students and colleagues and friends have done me the singular honor of reading this entire manuscript in one form or another. I am especially touched to be able to record a debt of thanks to Jeannie Alexander, Michael Bevers, Kat Curran, Agnes Heller, Bruce Lawrence, Mike Lippman, Anathea Portier-Young, Jeffrey Stout, and Jim Winchester for doing so.

Two debts of an entirely different order bear mentioning, though I would need to be virtually a painter and a poet at once to capture the essence of the thing. Alas, I am neither.

Lori Anne Ferrell has been a friend and fellow-traveler since our fortuitous meeting not long after the landscape of our country and of my garden began to change. She has read no fewer than seven complete drafts of this book and has commented upon each with wizened and loving intelligence, tending to my thoughts at every stage with patience and rare grace, almost as if they were her own. They often are. I remain in possession of several letters that concern those earlier drafts, and which succeed in creating the kind of shattering beauty I was aiming at then. Lori Anne is far more than the ideal reader, though she is that, too; she is actually that rarest of beings, the like-minded and supremely selfless friend. I count myself both blessed and nourished by her friendship.

As my professional life sauntered with agonizing slowness on its wide-wandering way to eventual permanent employment, and as I logged more miles in commute than I care to recount, it has taken more than a garden to keep me anchored to a place and rooted to a people. This book concludes with a long rumination on friendship, and I have been richly, shamelessly fortunate in this as well. Jim Winchester and Eve Lackritz,

Melanie Pavich, Larry Slutsker and Barbara Marston, Tim Craker and Mary Potter, and now an impressive host of children, young and not so young—Sophie and Adrian, Emma and Sarah, Michael and Oscar—have, in the sterling constancy of their affections, been a form of home to me, and all of them have turned their homes into places where my heart comes to rest. I am more grateful to them than I can properly say.

LAR
Summer Solstice 2007
Rome

Preliminaries:
Counting Costs

There is no better way [*hodos*], nor can there be, than the way whose lover I have always aspired to be, though she has broken with me many times, leaving me alone and unable to find my own way [*aporon*]. . . . It's not hard to point her out, but she's a very hard road to follow. Yet all the things born of art [*technē*] come along her way, or they do not come at all. . . . It's a sacred gift to humanity—so it seems to me, at least—laid before us by the gods like some Prometheus with his glittering fire. . . .[1]

. . .

I once shared a bottle of wine with a Greek philosopher; not everybody can say that. He was a professor of philosophy at the state university in Athens, and we had been introduced by a mutual friend who was also an aspiring artist. From the perspective of our current troubles, it seems a happier and far more innocent age—though I realize now that then was a sort of political prelude to what we are facing now. It was 1989. The end of a cold war, and the prelude to a hot one.

Like Diogenes, preferring frank speech to politesse, the Greek philosopher was trying to communicate his dismay with North American politics, and with the restless culture ("time is money") that allegedly gave it birth. And I had to admit that he had a point. He observed our legislative process far more closely than I did, since he saw in it something that

1. Plato *Philebus* 16b–c.

I did not see: namely, the threat posed by well-meaning men and women casting votes and promoting policies with no real sense of their implications in more distant parts of the world. *His* world, the Older one.

"The problem with you Americans," he noted with a sad smile, "is that you don't know how to count."

Eyebrow arched, and a little defensive, I poured another glass from the carafe and asked him what he meant.

"You lack patience," he explained. "You don't take the time to think what numbers mean."

I was still a little defensive, and still unclear about where he was headed with all this. Until he illustrated what he had in mind with an example. He told me that he saw no real evidence that we understand the difference between a million and a billion.

"Three more zeroes," I quipped. But he didn't laugh.

Numbers, I was learning, were a very serious business to Greek philosophers. And then came his example, and all desire I'd ever felt to joke with him evaporated in shock and dismay. I was stunned into a silence by it, almost embarrassed by the magnitude of what he saw so clearly, and I did not. Using time for his example, the philosopher merely counted seconds for me, piled them up into massive accumulations called minutes and hours, days and months, and more. Just that.

One *million* seconds, the philosopher patiently explained to me, is roughly ten days long.

One *billion* seconds—he paused here, for dramatic emphasis—is thirty-two *years*.

And *that* is the difference between a million and a billion. Some differences are so large that they seem almost moral—they become qualitative differences, not merely quantitative ones. Done properly, he warned me, there is a moral discipline that comes with counting well.

Gasping at first, then gulping down my wine, I clearly had to admit that he had a point. For, if I'm to be honest—with myself, and only latterly with him—then I have to admit that I don't always pay close enough attention to congressional debates about defense appropriations, don't attend sufficiently to whether they said that latest airplane or missile system will cost so-many millions, or billions, of dollars. Sometimes, the zeroes that are supposed to hold their places slip. And that marks a difference that makes a difference. A real one.[2]

Plato speaks to this kind of attention in the *Philebus*; he speaks of paying closer and more careful attention to numbers, as one key to living the very best and wisest kind of human life. It's all-too-easy, he warns, to speak casually of "infinity," of the things "too numerous to count." For related reasons, it's easy to throw up your hands in powerlessness, or despair. What is difficult—because it is a labor of love, and love is risky and difficult, and fraught with the possibility of pain—is to take the time to be careful with our numbers . . . to move, slowly, from one, to two, to many, to the count-less-ly large, and finally to that which has no limit and thus cannot be counted. It takes a very long time to get to a million, and a billion may seem forever far away. It takes a lot of moral energy and careful reflection to make such words and the ideas they represent feel real. That's the road Socrates tried to travel, come what may. He counted virtually every step he took. Plato emphasized what he considered to be a "science of numbering" in several of his later dialogues,[3] and Aristotle agreed with the Platonic insight that humans are the wisest of all animals precisely because they know how to number.[4] So said the Greek philosopher to me. I have not forgotten him.

But there can be a romance in that kind of remembering, a nostalgia in all those numbers. The danger in this story, the danger lurking behind a lot of stories—and it's compounded by the way I've chosen to remember, and thus to tell, this one—is that we romanticize them in retrospect. After all, what was I really expected to *do* with the philosopher's careful warning? Take the time to count to a million, slowly, by ones? Or throw up my hands in well-intentioned Liberal despair? What is an appropriate relationship to numbers, in the modern world, where we are constantly bombarded by piles of them too large and far-away-seeming to count? If I cannot really imagine a billion, then what can trillion, or a google, possibly mean?

---

2. As I write this last bit, estimates of the full cost of the Second Gulf War, to date—and just to North Americans—range between one-half and two trillion (that's with a *T*) dollars. Translated into seconds, that's enough time to take us back to the time of the Neanderthals. We clearly could do with some more precise counting here . . .

3. Plato *Epinomis* 677, and *Republic* 525d–e.

4. Aristotle *Problemata* xxx.6 (956a11–13).

Numbers play a funny role in the Bible, as we will see. Strangely, there's even a biblical book *called* "Numbers"—at least that's its name in English—so-called because of the weird ancient census laid out in its first four chapters. The book describes an attempt to count up, and so to account for, all of these people, the partial descendants of Abraham, the ones who were traced through the lineage of one of his grandsons, the one named Jacob. Or Israel—it depends. God tells Moses to count the people, to give them each a number. This is a *very* strange command, since it ought to be impossible. For this same God, in the very Book I'll be trying to read in this one, warned that such a task would ultimately be impossible. God promised Abraham, whose wife had not yet borne a son, that he would have so many descendants that they would be as un-countable as the stars in the sky,[5] or grains of sand by the seaside.[6] So why in the world would this same God tell Moses to count the people—people who are presumably too numerous to count? It seems an even stranger command in light of a later biblical story. Apparently King David ordered a census of his people[7]—or rather, Satan tempted him to do it—and by the time he'd counted one and a half million souls, God struck down seventy thousand of them with a plague. What is the lesson here? To stop counting? At a million? Or one? (Toward the end of this book, I'll make a cautious plea for the value of taking census, now and again—there's a local man I got to know that way).

A later Jewish prophet, Joshua the son of Joseph (we call him Jesus, of course), complicates the problem even more in what seems like a partial attempt to answer it. He assured his friends that God not only sees everything; God *counts* everything. "Even the hairs on your head are numbered," he smiles reassuringly.[8] Each of our hairs—like each one of us—has been counted, counted by God. Now, I suppose you could reasonably conclude that God knows how to count a lot better than people do. I suppose you could say that God has more brainpower, a far wider and longer point-of-view. But what, then, was the Greek *philosopher* saying in his eloquent plea to me? He was calling for more careful kinds of *human* counting. But what does learning how to count really get for us?

5. Gen 15:5.
6. Gen 22:17.
7. 1 Chr 21:1–14.
8. Matt 10:30.

In this book, I'll be aiming at these and similar philosophical lessons—lessons having to do with patience, and humility, and careful questions, but I'll be drawing them from a very different arena. Not from philosophy *per se*, but rather from a garden and from a Book. The idea came to me—exploded over me, really—five years ago. Let me try to explain how that happened first, by way of beginning.

When two towers twinned and dedicated to that most curious and long-lasting of all imperial ambitions, ancient or modern—something we call "world trade"—collapsed, then a distinctly North American kind of innocence was said to have collapsed with them. No longer do we seem to be befuddled yet well-meaning "innocents abroad": the guilty have come to live among us; and when we go abroad, we are no longer innocent. It has been a strange, and sad, and surreal time, and I suspect few of us in the United States have really recovered from the shock of it all. Surely our politics have not, although I continue to hope that they will, quietly, with more time.

I am one of those who lives several months out of each year abroad—primarily in Italy and in Greece. I had been asked to lead a seminar for three months, on a topic chosen for me by my colleagues at the Ionian University of Corfu. The topic was chosen in the immediate wake of that disaster as a teacherly response to the apparent delight at justice rendered that was expressed by an astonishing number of otherwise thoughtful Greek undergraduates. We miss something important if we fail to see, or else merely dismiss out-of-hand, just how violently we are resented, in many places around the world.

I entitled the course "The Other Americas," and in it we read some important North American fiction (*Huckleberry Finn* by Mark Twain, *Another Roadside Attraction* by Tom Robbins, *Gravity's Rainbow* by Thomas Pynchon, and *Jazz* by Toni Morrison) as a cultural invitation into some of the singular complexities and peculiarities of North American culture—American race relations, and American religious life, mostly. My aim for the seminar was fairly simple. I wanted to complicate, at least a little, the mental picture of "America" and "Americans" that most *non*-Americans have unwittingly assembled in their minds. When an anti-American protester burns a U.S. flag, for instance, what is he or she really trying to eradicate? It seems important, symbolically important, that the U.S. flag is the *only* national symbol I know that is *designed to change*. The U.S. flag actually has change built into it: with each new state, a new star appears on that vast blue background and its symbolic constellation of a country-forever-in-the-making. Some other countries that were also born of revolution—most notably, Greece herself—referenced that flag in the creation of their own. But in the nineteenth century, far more fledgling democracies born out of revolution appealed to the French tricolor—that inspired *alternative* symbol of revolution and political emancipation. (There may be a good reason for this: there is a strong suggestion that the design of the U.S. flag was originally inspired by the British East India Company's ensign—more on that shocker shortly). Still, the U.S. flag is a uniquely malleable symbol of a country—and a culture—which is very much aware of its own changeableness. The country itself is *designed* to change—not just to innovate, but actually to respond to the ever-changing face of its inhabitants and their various homeland cultures. The United States of America was thus intended to be a work always in process, never finished, and its flag was designed to say as much. So, why in the world burn *that*? Such questions become inescapable in the wake of what is surely one of the single greatest acts of iconoclasm the world has ever seen.

Iconoclasm often hides, and sometimes even erases, its true motives. When "terrorists" and other objectionists wage their blind warfare on that strange, fictional monster called "America," what do they really have in mind? How do they envision this entity, this "America?" Are they thinking of African-Americans? Chinese-Americans? Muslim-Americans? New-Agers? Hippies? Dropouts? Beats? Representatives of the counter-culture? Jazz musicians? Baseball players? Rock stars? Film stars? Computer moguls, and other billionaires? American-ness is not one thing, any more than Judaism, Christianity, or Islam are. Surely those who wish to wage war on "America" have in the front of *their* minds images of strong and serious soldiers in battle fatigues and black boots, working feverishly at military bases in places we seldom imagine them in—like Crete, like Saudi Arabia, like the Philippines. That's why the Pentagon was a target. But they probably also imagine the archetypal American financier—men and women who wheel and deal and move much too fast from millions to billions to trillions. That's why the World Trade Center was a target. "American" has been reduced in many minds to these two images, images of military and economic power. Yet their failure of imagination is tied, in some important ways, to our own. And therein lies a tale.

I first came to this topic here in Corfu, gazing out across a lovely stretch of Ionian waterway to the enormous and extraordinarily pretty Venetian fortress that dominates the harbor and the skyline of Corfu-town, some fifteen miles away from the home in which I lived. Across that waterway I am staring at the hills of either Greece or Albania—it's hard to say, because borders are so very much more fluid than the modern nation-state has traditionally allowed them to be. I spent three months there, alternately gazing across at that fortress, working in Corfu's magnificent imperial archives that are housed within it, and grappling with the complexities of our collective seminar and my own grief. But I kept coming back to the Venetians, musing over that lovely fortress on a hill, a setting for concerts and scholarly endeavors now, not for fireworks.

As anyone who has traveled in the eastern Mediterranean knows, the Venetians achieved an enormous and far-flung empire, one that is very hard to square with the site or shape or size of that ethereal, floating city. Venetian fortifications stretch from here on Corfu all the way to Cyprus and beyond. But how in the world did they *do* it? With some bemusement, and a great deal of pondering, I realize now that the Venetians achieved most of this *un*intentionally, and largely by accident. I have been very much preoccupied with this fact, the absolute and inescapable paradox of imperialism, ancient or modern. *Empires come by accident.*

A great many imperials have made their way across the gorgeous corridors of Corfu. The Romans came here and built their imperial villas. Nero had one built up on the northeast tip of the island. The Franks and Venetians came here and built their fortifications. The French came. The British came . . . and then finally "gave" all of these precious Ionian islands—the so-called *Heptanisia*, or "Seven Islands" (Corfu, Paxos, Antipaxos, Lefkada, Kephallonia, Zakynthos, and Odysseus's fabled home at Ithaka)—to the fledgling Greek nation in 1863, as a sort of present (!) from one royal household to another. This gift was formalized right here, on Corfu, in an old parliamentary building whose marble plaque still commemorates the deed and the day.

None of these empires—not the Roman, not the Venetian, not the French, not the British—were really created with a prior plan in mind. In fact, the most intentional and deliberate act of empire-construction was also the shortest-lived: the vast imperial construction of Napoleon, the one that finally put an end to Venice's empire in 1797. Napoleon was a prodigious dismantler, but the mantle he wished to replace it with fled from him, very much like his wife's sometime affections, almost right away.

Empires, it seems, happen almost by chance, develop through happenstance, and grow with an episodic and spastic internal rhythm. Empires usually grow out of a prior economic expansion and the creation of far-flung coastal emporia. They seem simply to happen, since human societies, like nature, abhor a vacuum.

It is only *after* empires happen economically that their quasi-creators wake up to the reality of what they have achieved. At *some* point, *some* Romans realized that, lo and behold, they had created a vast, pan-Mediterranean empire. Now all the harder questions commence: What are we *to do* with it? How are we to *organize* it? And *protect* it? Who should actually *run* it? In Rome, these questions erupted into civil war, the rise of the Caesars, and the death of the Roman Republic. The Venetians sailed along a slightly different tack, since they had resolved themselves to imperial politics and the leadership of a single man, the Doge, at a fairly early date. Far more importantly, the Venetians actually *invented* the tradition of permanent consulates and embassies in all the major cities with which they were then in contact. (Machiavelli was an "ambassador," of sorts, for Florence, but he traveled from city to city, whereas Venetian ambassadors were *permanently* installed in theirs). The Venetians understood that one runs an empire much as one runs a business, because empires *are* a business—through diplomacy and bureaucratic negotiation, as well as through an impressive ring of well-fortified harbors, through which their trade was filtered. The British unwittingly perfected this imperial art—in India, if not the Americas. In India, after the compromise of 1784, the East India Company and the British Crown actually *shared* in the governance of that golden and long-suffering colony.[9] So market capitalism and imperial politics were married once and for all.

I continue to believe and to hope that the awful carnage created in New York City several years ago may yet serve as a cruel wake-up call to us latter-day North American imperials, however unwitting and unwilling we also are. With thoughtfulness and prudence and some degree of

---

9. Anthony Wild's *East India Company* offers a stunning visual catalogue of that Company's long and ambiguous history.

calm, we may yet find fresh ways to imagine what we actually wish to do with what we have unwittingly managed to create around the world. Can we imagine an empire without killing a republic? Can we be truly democratic with so many men in arms on a permanent basis stationed all over the world? It would be a very fine thing for us to be more deliberate, and more patient, in examining such questions, especially in such a time as this. We ought to count our troops, not our surges, and we ought always to remain mindful of human costs.

The dramatic events of these not-so-long-ago years decisively altered my own identity as a teacher, even before I came to Corfu. I would not have been teaching a course called "The Other Americas" in Greece but for these tragic events, as general interest in the Americas and their history is otherwise fairly limited there. But even before I left the United States in April, my curricular identity at home had already been changed by happenstance to meet the moment and its peculiar needs. I changed my entire list of spring courses, offering seminars on Islam and its singularly complicated relationship to the Modern West. The idea was to provide myself and my students with some introductory working-knowledge of Islam and Islamic history,[10] as well as to learn to look at ourselves with other eyes, to gaze at western achievements, western cultures, and western politics through lenses ground for us a little further to the east. The course proved to be wonderfully cathartic—for its instructor and, I hope, for some of its students, too.

Our primary resource was an enormous, three-volume work entitled *The Venture of Islam*, written by the much-loved director of a graduate program in Islamic Studies at the University of Chicago. Marshall G. S. Hodgson was by all accounts a remarkable man, a deeply committed Quaker, and an astonishingly prodigious researcher. He landed on his life's work at a remarkably early age—he was scarcely twenty—learned all the requisite languages, started reading, started writing, and started thinking. He never stopped. He worked on *The Venture* right up until his premature death on a Chicago running track, where he suffered a massive heart attack in a wicked Midwest heat wave, and thus the all-important third volume of that life's work was published posthumously, without his having had the chance to revise it. It is a massive and really quite

---

10. I offered a lecture on this topic the following spring at the Ionian University, entitled "Islam kai ê simerinê Dusê" ("Islam and the Modern West").

moving undertaking, the intentional creation of a veritable empire of the human mind. Hodgson was convinced that really to write the history of any global religion, or any seismic historical event, one must have the *entire* world map in mind. Every history is a piece of world history, just as every human being is a precious piece and representative of humanity. Hodgson was a Quaker, a humanist, and an Islamicist of the very first rank. His life's work was an attempt to achieve a synthesis of the three—his Christianity, his commitment to the human cause, his abiding interest in Islam. His book is still *the* resource that ought to be on the bookshelf of any North American who has finally come to the realization that the part of the world we need desperately to begin to comprehend, and have not yet begun, is the vast world of Islam—stretching, as Hodgson put it, from "the Nile-to-Oxus" river basins. This, the so-called "Middle East"—not India, not China, not Japan—this is where our immediate and more mediate political future clearly lies. And that, I think, was the wake-up call that we all ought to have received on the 11th of September some years ago. Instead, we have contributed to the increasing radicalization of a geographical zone that now runs from western Pakistan all the way to the Mediterranean Sea.

In a brilliant initial description of the pre-Islamic culture of the Arabian peninsula, dominated by camel-nomads (this is just what *'arab* means, in their language, apparently) and the towns on which they alternately fed or served ("raiding and trading," as he puts it, can actually *be* a way of life), Hodgson offers a marvelous and telling description of the religious self-understanding of the Prophet Muhammad. It is so profound that we spent nearly two hours working through it in our seminar. It echoes a point made several times in the Qur'an,[11] and it calls our attention to the biblical patriarch *par excellence*: Abraham.

> In the quarrel with the Jews it became clear that Islam not only was distinct from paganism but, even within monotheism, formed an independent religious system, parallel and distinct from Judaism and Christianity. Whereas up to this point Muhammad had expected his cult to conform by and large to that of the Jews (for instance in praying toward Jerusalem and in observing certain fasts), now the Muslim was set off markedly. Learning that Abraham was considered the common ancestor of Israelites and

---

11. Qur'an 2:135–38 and 3:65–70.

of Ishmaelite Arabs, he pointed out *that Abraham was faithful to God though he was neither Jewish nor Christian*, having lived before either Moses or Jesus. Muhammad's cult was to be like that of Abraham.[12]

Abraham, the biblical patriarch. Abraham, the alleged founder of three scriptural monotheisms. I say "alleged" because, as Hodgson's description of the Qur'an's conception of Abraham makes abundantly clear, he was not the founder of a *tradition*, but of a *faith*. "Pure religion need be bound by no communal limitations—as Abraham himself was bound by none."[13] That freedom from institutional affiliation would be crucial. It still is, in what may seem to many North Americans a remarkably decentralized faith such as Islam.

This is a very easy paradox to miss: Abraham may be considered the father of all three scriptural monotheisms (the "people of the Book," as the Qur'an puts it), but he was a monotheist who never had a scripture. Moses would not come along for five hundred years or more, leaving the Torah and the Law behind. Jesus came along perhaps fifteen hundred years after that, leaving the Gospel in his God-inspired wake. And Muhammad followed next, some six hundred years later still. The Qur'an makes a great deal of these time-lags: "Impatience is the very stuff man is made of," it proclaims . . . ,[14] but God is patient, and enduring—like Abraham.

Any time my students tell me that they are "not religious," but "feel very spiritual," I think this is partly what they're aiming at, trying to find a way to say. A great many thoughtful people have sat for too long at the tables of organized religion, only to walk away disappointed and still famished. The spiritual hunger within Christendom and Islamdom is real. A similar spiritual hunger was percolating in Roman society in the eastern Mediterranean in the generations surrounding Jesus' journeying, and such ferment was equally characteristic of the semi-nomadic Arabian peninsula in the age of Muhammad. This spiritual ferment often gives birth to new religions, but these religions tend to see themselves as rooted both in the vague and unformed spirituality, as well as the tolerant henotheism, of Abraham. You must go backward to go forward, you need

12. Hodgson, *Venture of Islam*, 3:178; italics mine.
13. Ibid.
14. Qur'an 21:37.

history to travel well toward any territory worth the trouble of exploration. There is food for thought here, as well as substance for a real, rather than superficial, rapprochement between Christianity and Islam on this very point. If it all began with Abraham, then Abraham is a symbol of faith *before* its institutionalization. Abraham paints a picture of what the spark of divine revelation kindled, before it cooled and congealed into its more predictable and traditional modes, forms that are related to the original spark much as dark embers are related to roaring flames. You can use such things to start a fire again, but it takes real effort. And it's dangerous, unless you're very careful. There is a lot to worry about where Abraham is concerned, as I will try to show.

Abraham was a desert wanderer, a true journeyman, a Godward mystic. Tom Robbins, who is a hilariously astute observer of the North American counter-culture, one whom we read in the seminar I led on Corfu, referred to true mysticism as "the science of godward solutions."[15] I like that phrase, and it is hardly unique to the U.S. counter-culture. It is echoed by Philo, a thoroughly Hellenized Jew from Alexandria to whom I will refer many times in this book (admittedly, Philo was a far more important figure for Christians who found him congenial, than he was to Jews and Muslims, who often did not). Philo wrote an enormous amount of Platonic allegorizing in Greek, in the generation before several traumatic Christian events so thoroughly jolted the Jewish mainstream into a different kind of "orthodoxy." Philo, for his part, imagined Abraham in much the same way the Qur'an does: he was schooled in "Godward things."[16] So Abraham is ultimately a mystery. And in the end, Abraham is also where this, my book, is headed.

After the somewhat shocking chit-chat with a Greek philosopher, the idea for this book began with a question: How should a reflective citizen of the United States of America—one committed to a more serious form of democracy and probably better described as spiritual rather than religious—try to comprehend the awful accumulation of events over the last five years? How should he or she respond to the unwitting creation of a far-flung and truly global American emporium/empire? For that is what many persons in the Islamic world, in particular, have been trying to tell us: that we *have* wittingly or unwittingly created an empire, and

---

15. Robbins, *Another Roadside Attraction*, 112.

16. The Greek says *ta pros ton Theon*, a lovely phrase that may be found in an allegorical meditation entitled *On the Migration of Abraham* [Peri Apoikias] Book III, §81.

that its commitment to good or ill remains highly uncertain. And while I know that it will not do to describe the current situation as if all Muslims speak with one voice, or as if all Americans are imperialistic, there is a subtler point here, one worthy of our continued reflection and attention. But what does all this have to do with religion? More specifically, what does it have to do with Judaism, Christianity, and Islam? Can Jews and Christians and Muslims talk meaningfully *together* about what has happened, and what continues to happen, around the world today?

As bizarre as it may seem at this juncture, *this* North American responded in two ways, once he'd gotten his teaching affairs in order, and managed to find his feet. I went back to the book of Genesis, and I went back to my garden.

Yet I began these ruminations by recalling a conversation with a Greek philosopher; that's important as well. The complicating truth of the matter is that I took these speculative trips—back to my garden and back to the Book—inspired by the same tradition that inspired Philo some two thousand years ago: Plato and the Greek poets. That vast Greek tradition of literature and philosophy will be a recurrent theme, and really a sort of lodestar, in this book as well. All of the arts, the truly creative human technologies or *technai*, says Plato, come in two forms.[17] One of them concerns itself with the care, what he calls the *therapeia*, of mortal things, things that are bodies, bodies that die. It's a vast art of managing mortality, in a way. The other truly creative human activity has to do with the way we gather, or mold, or imitate such things. (That's not a bad definition for religion, too.) Caring and tending and imitation: a good gardener is an artist; and a good garden goes "Godward." In another dialogue to which I have already referred, Plato suggests that the seasons of the earth, and all of the manifold natural beauties she contains, come about when the infinite "gets mixed up" with finite things.[18] Sorting out these complex Platonic themes, moving from one, through many, counting all the way to the limits of things . . . this marks the supreme way of life to which Socrates tells us he has committed himself. It doesn't take a very large leap of poetic imagination to see natural beauty, then, as a harmonious marriage of an eternal God with mortal beings. Plato himself makes this connection pretty plainly, in ways that still perplex those who continue

---

17. Plato *Sophist* 219a–b.
18. Plato *Philebus* 26a–b.

to insist on thinking of him merely as a "pagan," and yet that inspired those (like Philo, or Marsilio Ficino, the great Florentine theologian of the Renaissance) who saw Plato fundamentally as a theologian. He was both. And neither. Like a lot of people.

So we garden, similarly to the way we think, and in so doing, we bring into being what did not exist before. Like God, we create. We create beauty. We make ideas. We put all of this into words. It is as pure as it is simple: we humans make things. And if we are very, very fortunate, then we find ways to tend to our thinking while we tend to our gardens. I am so fortunate. And a description of appropriate gratitude is a part of what I'm after in this book, too.

In the autumn of 2001, I returned to my garden. There's a rich Renaissance tradition of doing precisely this, one that makes the garden the very fittest place for meditating on decisive matters of war, and of peace. Even Machiavelli imagined his famous discourse on the *Art of War* simply as a conversation among friends, a conversation that took place in a traditional Renaissance garden.[19] The Italian villa and the Renaissance garden became matters of renewed North American interest around the turn of the twentieth century, thanks to the influence of Charles A. Platt's *Italian Gardens* in 1894, and still more to Edith Wharton's 1904 classic, *Italian Villas and their Gardens*; these books were to leave a deep impression on the culture and culminated in the classicizing democratic philosophy we see in the public landscaping of Frederick Law Olmsted. Gardens and parks became matters of great public concern, and public funding, in twentieth-century North America, and gardening books became at least as popular, if not more popular, than biblical meditations. This book will attempt to weave those two popular genres together. But there is, and presumably always was, a subtext to this: the renewed fascination with Renaissance gardens was also emblematic of a fascination with "wildness" and *pagan* space. Gardens were imagined to be where Pan lived.[20] Despite Plutarch's and Pascal's famous disclaimers, Pan was thought to be very much alive—and hiding out in a garden.

---

19. For more on the Italian villa and sculpture garden, see Impey and MacGregor, eds., *Garden and Grove*, Coffin, *Villa in the Life of Renaissance Rome*, Strong, *Renaissance Garden*, as well as the exhibition guide, *Villa in Italia*.

20. For a lovely meditation on the connection between gardening and its neoclassical, pagan resonance, see John Hanson Mitchell's *Wildest Place on Earth*, 25–26, 63–69.

Still, I did not simply garden, and I was not looking for Pan, at least not consciously. I also went back to Genesis, because primordial peace, according to the Book, was born in a garden as well. So I went back a little further, back to the story of God's (unwitting?) creation of an enormous opportunity and an enormous problem: human being. Then I moved forward, or at least I *tried* to do so, to find a way back to Abraham, back to the mystery-man who started it all. I meditated on all of this, sought counsel and insight, found the time really to think about it and to count my steps, in my own garden. This little book is what came up in that strange soil.

LAR
Corfu, GREECE

I want time to pool, not race, but tonight I'm madly impatient for the growing season to begin, and the garden, which is a different Eden for every gardener, to reinvent itself as a renewable paradise, if not a permanent one. I don't believe in garden gods, but I do believe in the power of invocation to stir the spirit. Garden of growth, garden of green blood, garden where dappled light and water mix in the trees, crow garden, beetle garden, garden of dreams, garden on the oasis of a life-drenched planet, garden where desire finds form, garden of floral architecture and speckled fawns, garden where wonder is incised on a pebble millions of years old, garden visibly and invisibly teeming, garden of beds and seed parlors, garden of dew and overdue, garden where we plight our troth and ply our trade, garden that tilts the mind into the sacred, fleeting garden, memorial garden, garden abuzz and atwitter, garden where toxins and tonics both thrive, pool garden, cloud garden, garden that's an urn for the soul, garden of roll calls and lists where life tests different recipes, garden where rain falls like manna, garden whose perennial borders are infinite, garden whose customs and taboos make mischief in the mind, garden of snow, mind garden, garden of quartz crystal and siren light.

Any day now spring will revive the blast-frozen valley, tune up the dawn chorus, and hymn the poplars with winter's end. . . . Spring is unlatching its heavy doors, rousting old dusty hibernators from their sleep, and beginning a quiet fumbling with buttons, knots and nubbins, and the bolting ribbons of time, light, and gore. As I walk down to the mailbox, enveloped in mist, birds snitch on twitchy feet in the aspens, morning ghosts between the houses, and the air tastes green at last.

Diane Ackerman, *Cultivating Delight*

chapter one

SOIL

In contrast to commercial farmers, organic gardeners practice a so-called golden rule of organic gardening that declares we put back into the soil everything we take out. Any gardener who practices this rule soon learns that he or she is not so much growing produce as growing soil. The result is that the organic garden is perhaps best understood as a soil garden. The idea is important enough to deserve repeating: although the organic garden is often described as a place where chemical pesticides and fertilizers are verboten (which is true), in fact it is the place human beings grow soil. Farsighted organic gardeners grow soil so that plants, home, nation, and even planet may prosper. Our revisionist history of the soil lauds organic gardening as one of life's best tutors for teaching a sense of place.

Most organic gardeners would probably agree that the modern farmer *had* to destroy the soil. This conclusion seems all but obvious from even a cursory examination of farm practices over the past two hundred years. A disrespect for the soil was built into the American farm system from the very start. It was perhaps exemplified by the mythical nineteenth-century farmer *bragging* that he'd used up three or four farms in a lifetime. This legendary strong-willed man is the farmer's analogue to the logger's Paul Bunyan clear-cutting entire bioregions, the analogue to the rancher's Pecos Bill leading millions of cattle to tromp over virgin watersheds all across the American West.

These are a few of the more famous historical archetypes of the American dream.[1]

...

It's cool this morning, not unusually so, but it feels unusual, given how hot it has been recently. Hard not to think of global warming, and other global worries, on shortening days like this, especially when they stay so hot. Passing over the long-anticipated, luxurious, and infinitely gentle transitions that normally characterize autumnal life in Atlanta, this fall seems to have stolen in on us overnight. The steam rising off of my coffee cup is visible even against the grey canopy of morning sky. It is cold. And it is quiet—due, in part, to the fact that the Atlanta Braves were playing baseball until quite late again last night. The city, groggy after yet another ballgame that lasted 'til well past midnight, seems still to be sleeping it off. There's a lot to sleep off, this time. For the Braves have been by far the most dominant and the most consistent team in the major leagues over the past decade, and more. Most of that has been due to their superb pitching staff—subtle and precise, sometimes overpowering, altogether *nonpareil*. The team has qualified for post-season championship play the last eleven years in a row. But they have only won a single World Series: a glorious affair, concluded here at home, in Atlanta—at the old Fulton County stadium, where a remarkably strong-handed African-American from Alabama by the name of Henry Louis Aaron shattered Babe Ruth's lifetime home run record in 1974—not so very long before the Olympic Games came to the city, and left a new stadium in their wake. Sadly, this year's drama was more in line with the ending Atlantans have begun to expect. The team posted the best record in the major leagues this year and had seemed, at times, a juggernaut almost impossible to resist. Yet we have been eliminated again in the first round of post-season play, after a nail-biting final inning of the final game, one in which the winning run came to the plate with no one out, and still our team failed to score. There will be much to mull over this morning, and alas, across the long winter months ahead of us.

1. Nollman, *Why We Garden*, 69.

Being a Braves fan consists, at least partly, in consenting to live inside of an opera, to live in the face of seemingly continual disappointment. Hope endlessly deferred. And, here's the trick, the experience of this can be *beautiful*.[2] I know that die-hard Red Sox fans in Boston say the same thing—or at least they used to—and perhaps with greater justification. But with less justice. Disappointment, defeat, and dashed hopes simply play differently here, in the south. Boston was never burned to a cinder in wartime. Boston never fought a war it later regretted—until now. The city of Boston trades in national myths, not original sins. For that kind of pathos, and that kind of dramatic intensity, you've simply got to go south. As I have done. It has proven to be a good place for beginning again.[3] That has become an important idea to me; it is an important idea in the Book, too.

So a groggy city sleeps on, sleeps off its disappointment, and awakes to a new season. In the silence, I notice pigeons gently cooing and playing on the rooftops. A dog barks somewhere up the street. My stomach gurgles as I sip coffee—the gentle nectar that turns waking into such a subtle, quiet pleasure. In the garden.

I am here, as I am here nearly every day over morning coffee, to survey the subtle changes that evening brings in this season. I want to see whether the latest seedlings have crested the surface yet, to see what vegetables are ripe and ready for picking, what plants need trimming back, what beds need fresh weeding; I pay special care to attend to the younger shoots. It's become a point of pride that I use neither fertilizer of any kind, nor pesticides here; I have found that fresh grass clippings work best, both to hedge in the individual rows of various crops, and also to minimize the number of weeds that manage to muscle their way up into the sunlight. These clippings also serve to enrich the soil, as cut grass is gradually, almost magically, transformed with a little help from the veritable army of earthworms just below the surface—the very things the birds are after. Each morning I find the garden pockmarked like a miniature No Man's Land, the latest scars on the beds of grass clippings revealing dark earth below, a sure testimony to last night's skirmishes in the great, never-ending war. The birds poke rather spastically through the grass, looking for their breakfast. In the process, they often unwittingly

---

2. I have been much informed by Hans Ulrich Gumbrecht's marvelous *In Praise of Athletic Beauty* in seeing this.

3. For more on this notion, see "The South as Tragic Landscape."

bury my new plants under a deadly umbrella of heavy, wet grass. So, along with the savory smell of coffee, and the subtler aromas of the nearby spice garden wafting in on the breeze, I savor the feeling of damp bedding in my hands, and the cooler (especially this morning) feeling of young life, burrowing down and out, in search of moisture and firmer ground.

That magical transaction, from green to brownishblack, is a source of endless wonderment, and no little pride of place, for me. I am gazing now upon rich, loamy vegetable and flower beds that bear eloquent testimony to the constancy of my affections for this place over a fairly long stretch of years. Dearly loved friends have come into, then gone out of, my life here. Romantic love has faded; new love has graced me with its rejuvenating, always unexpected, and sustaining presence. Hardly a miracle-worker myself, I have nonetheless stood watchman over some truly miraculous transformations. I have been witness to, and perhaps occasionally even an agent in, the transformation of this impossible patch of red Georgia clay—which bakes all summer long no more than four inches below the surface—into a rich, loamy brown topsoil in the comparatively short space of a decade. Today, in the cool onset of morning-light, that rich soil is especially wet with autumn condensation, and a feeling of extraordinary promise. It smells to me very much like the outrageous fertility of nature herself. Yawning as I take another sip, I'm reminded of an old Turkish proverb I heard once in Istanbul: "Coffee should be black as hell, strong as death, and sweet as love." The same might be said for soil.

Hours too numerous to allow of any easy counting lie buried in this small piece of personal plotting. The place well embodies what Jim Nollman refers to as that "golden rule of organic gardening." We must grow *soil* before we can truly grow anything else worth growing. "Growing soil"—I like that image. And it's true for wine as well: neither French nor German nor Spanish nor Italian even have a word for wine-*making* . . . only wine-*growing*. It all goes back to the soil, the idea of *terroire*. Nollman's book speaks eloquently about an intriguing constellation of ideas that will interest me a great deal today: the sacred centrality of gardens; sweaty, manual labor; a light-footed and fairly unformed spirituality; and finally, the importance of the sense of *place* to the fullest realization of the potential in a human life. The rich loam in my garden runs two feet deep in the oldest beds now, the very first I cut and cultivated here in what seems almost to have been a former lifetime to me, now.

Over one third of a billion seconds (three hundred fifteen million, three hundred sixty thousand, to be exact) amounts to ten years. For ten long, steamy springs and summers, I have deposited and worked countless bags of grass clippings into the soil, just here. Countless hours have been spent doubled over this same piece of ground, weeding, cutting . . . and sweating, it seems important to add. For all its pretension to quiet and fallow rest, gardening is, at its times and in its seasons, pretty backbreaking work. Through all of this, I've also been simply watching, and looking, and listening. I know this piece of place probably better than I know any other in the world—with the possible exception of an old Hellenistic harbor in Crete called Phalasarna, where I excavated for six idyllic summers in the late 1980s and early 1990s. I dug there a great deal, but I did not garden; it makes a difference.

This bears thinking more about, this powerful attachment to *local* and *personal* place. I will make a great deal of it in this book, partly because the Bible so clearly does. It is also what gardeners know best, the knowledge they quest after, and the feeling they seek to pass on. I know every inch of ground in this place, have come to understand the peculiarities of every little microsystem. I know where plants do well, know where they seem inevitably to fail. I know the difference between one trench and its less-fertile neighbor no more than six inches closer to the sunrise. I know where the water tends to collect in the heavy rains of July, or October, just as I know, from one month to the next, when and where the sunlight will strike best. Finally, and perhaps most important, I know when it's time to leave the whole area alone for the space of two months, or more. This sacred winter sabbatical makes summer harvests possible again.

Literally hundreds of pounds of dark compost have been sponged into this soil as well, during this comparatively quiescent autumnal season—all of it slowly moldering and mutating in the sacred space of a small fenced enclosure I built several years ago, when I finally came to see the decisive importance of growing soil. It was just about this time of the year, I believe. Now I pick a spot each season—it seems like random chance, the purest spur of the moment, but I am sure that there is some deeply, darkly hidden plan behind every step—one bed to be freshly composted. It is fun—after all the careful springtime planning, decisions about what to plant, and where, and when, what new crops to try, what older crops to give up on—fun to let a kind of quiet chaos reign in the garden over our blessedly brief southern winters, the quiet that frames the solstice. That is a large portion of what the composting is for, I think: quiet and meditation, a kind of seasonal closure.

There is nothing terribly profound in these random morning meanderings; their personal poignancy derives solely from their proximity. Of course there is a more general, partly philosophical and partly ecological, pertinence in table scraps being churned slowly into next year's topsoil. "Consider compost," Diane Ackerman muses,

> To create it one transforms the waste products of the garden by digesting them (via bacteria) and turning them into rich dark stuff essential for further growth. If only we could cast off life's bad experiences that way, gather them in a pile at the edge of our awareness, where they're slowly digested and turned into personal growth.[4]

But there is an immediacy about this whole transaction, here, in a garden of one's own. Yesterday evening, for instance, I picked a wonderful batch of new garden beans. As I listened to the evening news, I cut off the tips and tore hard, stringy veins from their backs. Within thirty minutes of harvesting, these beans were simmering on the stove. Within an hour, they were steaming on a platter I set before several close friends. Within three hours, their fibrous leavings were back in the garden, one part of it, in any case, marked now as compost-in-the-making. It is this rich cycle—the sacred circle which ties life (fresh produce) to death (half-eaten castaways) to rebirth (new soil)—that one learns best to honor in a garden. Some images have an inescapably spiritual edge to them. Pay close enough attention to the rhythms in a garden, and you may find your own sense of the relation between life and death, the finite and the infinite, subtly changed as well. As the Qur'an puts it, in a *surah*, or chapter, entitled "The Greeks" (!): "He brings forth the living from the dead, and the dead from the living. *He resurrects the earth after its death.* Likewise you shall be raised."[5] Believing that, you may find your own relation to time and eternity changed, in some of the same ways the Greek philosopher pointed out to me.

---

4. Ackermann, *Cultivating Delight*, 86.
5. Qur'an 30:18–19, 50.

For time has an odd pace in a garden, unlike any I have known elsewhere. Gardens require a grand, an almost philosophical, patience as we wait for crops to ripen, anticipating their flavors, textures, scents for long months. But time has a stop-start quality here as well. Suddenly, it's all before you, ripe and ready for the picking. The garden's cadence is very much like the Bible's. And it occurs to me that it's lent a flavor even to the way I am writing about it—starting slow, looking for an opening, easing into a beginning. The real action comes almost before you realize it's happened.

God promised a man named Abram eventual ownership of an unspecified stretch of uncannily fertile, close-to-the-Mediterranean river valley. Yet it will take over seven hundred years, including a four-hundred year lacuna involving brutal enslavement in Egypt, before God delivers on these promises. The Bible, it would seem, takes a *very* long view of things. It takes the time to count. So does its God. And so does any gardener or vintner worthy of these sacred callings. After months of anticipation, and really all of a sudden, the produce is there, arriving not a little bit at a time, mind you, but in handfuls, bucketfuls, an embarrassing superabundance. All need for patience gone, time moves suddenly, summeringly, swiftly. Three hours separate a harvest from the compost, with a fresh feast in between. That is the marvel of the late summer and early fall, to a gardener. The food we eat returning, itself, to soil. As will I. As do we all.

The first human being was called Adam, says the Book. And *adamah* was the Hebrew word for soil. Human. Humus. Hmm.

chapter two

SUN

In the geographical survey, the course of the World's History has been marked out in its general features. The *Sun*—the Light—rises in the East. Light is simply self-involved existence; but though possessing thus in itself universality, it exists at the same time as an individuality in the Sun. Imagination has often pictured to itself the emotions of a blind man suddenly becoming possessed of sight, beholding the bright glimmering of the dawn, the growing light, and the flaming glory of the ascending Sun. The boundless forgetfulness of his individuality in this pure splendor, is his first feeling—utter astonishment. But when the Sun is risen, this astonishment is diminished; objects around are perceived, and from them the individual proceeds to the contemplation of his own inner being, and thereby the advance is made to the perception of the relation between the two. Then inactive contemplation is quitted for activity; by the close of day man has erected a building constructed from his own inner Sun; and when in the evening he contemplates this, he esteems it more highly than the original external Sun. For now he stands in a *conscious relation* to his Spirit, and therefore a *free* relation. If we hold this image fast in mind, we shall find it symbolizing the course of History, the great Day's work of Spirit.

The History of the World travels from East to West, for Europe is absolutely the end of History, Asia the beginning.[1]

---

1. Hegel, *Lectures on the Philosophy of History*, 103.

...

The sun is higher now, having crested the low rise of trees to the east. It will bestow a first kiss on the nearest plants in another quarter of an hour. Belying the bizarre chill of yesterday evening, and the lingering cool of first light, it will be hot again today. Underdressed for now, I retreat inside and linger over a fresh tomato eaten on homemade toast. The delicately acidic flavor, mingled with salt, and another taste I cannot quite identify but that has something to do with the fantastic miracle of fruition itself, prods me gently into wakefulness, along with a second cup of coffee. I have been eating a lot of tomatoes lately (and will return to this very important topic later on today), knowing that fresh ones will not be available for very much longer. The vines are browning faster now, against the slow, encroaching cold, and there are fewer new shoots every day—causing me to remember all-too-well how much I will long for a fresh tomato, say, in the cold melancholy of late February. This October has been so uncharacteristically warm that we will have a punishing late January and February, I am afraid. The grand give-and-take of natural justice. The Farmer's Almanac says the same. But I don't know this for reading it; I *feel* it somewhere in my bones, and in my spirit, not yet fully awake. I rarely bring books into my garden. That has always seemed important. If you pay attention to how the plants grow, and wither, and even how they die, you can tell a lot about what sort of weather is coming. It's almost as if they know.

God planted a garden. And that garden was "in the east." That is what the Book says. The Book doesn't say where. The Book doesn't say when. It just says *miqqedem*, "in the east."

Now, Hebrew is a very ancient language, as written languages go. It is an emphatically syllabic language, which is why the words tend to look and sound the way they do: one consonant and one vowel, another consonant and another vowel; it just goes on and on like that. And yet, even putting it this way is misleading. For Hebrew, *ancient* Hebrew, did not have vowels at all. They were implied, assumed and inserted by the language's earliest readers and writers. Archaic *Greek*, it would seem, was the first written language to have independent and symbolic vocalization, letters that stood for vowels, all by themselves.

Socrates makes a great deal of this literary innovation in several later Platonic dialogues.[2] He is interested in that marvelous human capacity we have already seen invoked several times, the gift for putting things together. The individual elements in our mixtures and combinations are unknowable, Socrates suggests, but the combinations themselves are (the Greek word for such combinations is *syllabôn*, from which we get our English word 'syllable'). In the case of a written language, the letters, or *grammata*, are the elements, and "syllables" are their combinations. But then Socrates makes the decisive point by looking at the first two letters of his own name: sigma (Σ) and omega (Ω). It may seem like a strange thing to focus on, to us, but it was obviously an important distinction to him. The seven vowels in ancient Greek (alpha, epsilon, eta, iota, omicron, umicron and omega) are called the letters with voices (*ta hepta phonên*), whereas the rest, the consonants, are called voiceless (*tôn aphonôn*). You can't really discern anything about them, can't find what Plato will call a *logos* for them, something that helps to explain what they are. But put them together with a vowel, and you get a combination, a syllable, something you can say, something you can say more about, something you can analyze. You don't really know what an *S* will be, Socrates suggests, until you give it a voice.[3] So it's the vowels that do the crucial work, which is why Plato calls them "the most energetic" (*enargestata*) of all the letters. Vowels quite literally breathe things into being. You don't know what a thing will be until it breathes.

Later, Socrates returns to this same idea in a justly famous myth about the Egyptian creation of writing by an ancient wise man, or a god, called Theuth.[4] Here the philosopher's concern is the one we met at the outset: that we not assume too quickly that things are numberless, and thus give up the sacred obligation to count them carefully and arrange them into some kind of an order. Socrates distinguishes between *three* kinds of letters, now: the voiced ones (*ta phôneenta*); the voiceless ones (*ta aphôna*); and the ones in the middle, which make a sound (*phthongê*) but have no real voice (*phônê*). This is a more complicated distinction,

---

2. This begins with the *Theaetetus* 203 a–c.
3. Aristotle says much the same thing in his *Poetics* 1456b20.
4. *Phaedrus* 274c–275b, and *Philebus* 18c–d.

but the main idea is still pretty clear. Voiced sound is limitless; it can be emitted and played with in a numberless variety of dialects, distinctions and deliveries. The human capacity for making sounds is singular . . . and countless. And yet when we speak, there are no spaces, no breaks, in between the letters and the words. *Spoken* language is one continuous flow, written on the wind (or, as Keats later put it in his epitaph, written on water). But *written* language is a system, a system of signs designed to break up the flow, and to systematize it. And in so doing, almost as if by a magic power, we can write syllables with letters that one may then read and turn into spoken words, again. It is the invention of the vowels, the letters with a *true* voice, which made this marvelous leap into Greek abstraction possible. And leap they surely did.

Anne Carson, who is a brilliant poet as well as a classicist and a philosopher,[5] draws out an interesting connection between this uncanny alphabetic innovation and the birth of the poetic and erotic life. Here is how she puts the point in a crisp, luminous meditation entitled *Eros the Bittersweet*:

> The Greeks created their alphabet by taking over the syllabic sign-system of the Phoenicians and modifying it in certain decisive ways sometime in the early eighth century B.C. It is standard to say that their chief modification amounted to "introducing the vowels." Vowels were not expressed in Phoenician writing, but from the outset the Greek alphabet had five vowels in full use. . . . A script that furnishes a true alphabet for a language is one able to symbolize the phonemes of the language exhaustively, unambiguously and economically. The first and only ancient sign system to do so was the Greek alphabet.[6]

But why are vowels of such decisive importance to the poet-philosopher? This claim will sound funny when you first hear it, but it is really all because of love. "Oral cultures and literate cultures," she says, "do not think, perceive or fall in love in the same way."[7] And a lover who has full control of her vowels—well now, that is something else. It's a deeply meditative notion, involving a whole new attention to the breath.

5. For an essay summarizing Carson's entire body of work, see my essay, "Righting the Self and Writing God."
6. Carson, *Eros the Bittersweet*, 53.
7. Ibid., 42.

> [V]owels are inconceivable without a prior, dashing innovation. For the components of every linguistic noise are two: (1) a sound . . . ; and (2) the starting and stopping of the sound. . . . The actions that start and stop sounds, which we think of as "consonants," can by themselves produce no sound. They are nonsounds having, as Plato said, "no voice." . . . When we think about this remarkable invention of the Greek alphabet and think about how a human mind operates when it uses the alphabet, the remarkable operations of *eros* stand forward for comparison. . . . Here at the entrance to written language and literate thinking we see that analogy revivified by the archaic writers who first ventured to record their poems. The alphabet they used was a unique instrument. Its uniqueness unfolds directly from its power *to mark the edges of sound*.[8]

And why are these so-called *edges* of such decisive importance? In a word, because of the power and perplexing quality of human desire. You need the clear perception of an edge in order to desire anything apart from your self. And you need to mark that edge to be able to love it, to be capable of falling into love at all.

> Eros is an issue of boundaries. He exists because certain boundaries do. In the interval between reach and grasp, between glance and counterglance, between "I love you" and "I love you too," the absent presence of desire comes alive. But the boundaries of time and glance and I love you are only aftershocks of the main, inevitable boundary that creates Eros: the boundary of flesh and self between you and me. And it is only, suddenly, at the moment when I would dissolve that boundary, I realize I never can. . . .
>
> If we follow the trajectory of eros we consistently find it tracing this same route: it moves out from the lover toward the beloved, then ricochets back to the lover himself and the hole in him, unnoticed before. Who is the real subject of most love poems? Not the beloved. It is that hole.[9]

She doesn't exactly confess this here, but Anne Carson has a sneaking suspicion that the people who invented this remarkable alphabetic ab-

---

8. Ibid., 54–55, italics mine.
9. Ibid., 30.

straction—the written vowel, the symbolic and systolic voice—also made possible, precisely by doing so, the new kinds of poetry at which Sappho and others immediately excelled: *love poetry*.[10] What she does say, and says with pretty eloquence, is that literacy—in this glorious new alphabet Sappho could compose in—will even change your perspective on *time*, if you permit it.[11] For speech is a phenomenon trapped in time; by the time I get to the second syllable of my own name, the first one has already disappeared into thin air. Writing freezes time by stopping the breath, keeps whole words together, and so provides a tantalizing glimpse or foretaste of what it would be like to control time—if only for a while. Scripts stop time; so do scriptures. They force us to slow down, to catch our breath.

Now, Hebrew doesn't work the way Greek does. Neither, for that matter, did ancient Phoenician, nor Linear A and Linear B, those mysterious early Bronze Age syllabaries from Crete and the Greek mainland that were finally deciphered several decades ago.[12] The Hebrew language works with *roots*, much as a gardener does. A verbal root in Hebrew is a set of three consonants that may be vocalized in many different ways to make nouns, verbs, adverbs, and the like. And since the vowels are not written down, the reader has to supply them. Given their common root, the relationship between a related set of words and ideas is often revealed in interesting and provocative ways in Hebrew—much like multiple shoots in the garden, springing up quite near to one another out of a single, originary bulb.

The Hebrew root I was noticing just now is *q-d-m*. It has an intriguing semantic range.[13] As a noun, a *masculine* noun, it is *qedem*, and it meant everything from "front," to "before," to, as we might expect, "the east." As a masculine plural, *qadôm*, the noun refers primarily to "the east wind(s)." When it is a verb, it is *qadam* (among countless other forms, of course, since verbs *move*), and it means "to come to the front," or "to be in front," as well as "to meet" (sometimes in a hostile or aggressive way, but not always). *Qidmath* is a sort of preposition, meaning "in front of," or

---

10. Ibid., 41. Carson's own intriguing translation of Sappho's fragmentary leavings finally appeared a few years ago, with the dazzling title *If Not, Winter*.

11. Carson, *Eros the Bittersweet*, 120–21.

12. John Chadwick's *Linear B and Related Scripts* offers up a fun description of the amateurs who were really responsible for making that happen.

13. In all of this discussion, I am entirely dependent on William Gesenius's masterful compendium, *A Hebrew and English Lexicon of the Old Testament*, especially 869–70.

"over against."[14] As an adverb, the word is *qidmah*, and when it is voiced this way it means "eastward" or "to the east." Interestingly enough, and related to this last idea, the *q-d-m* root may also be turned into a rarer sort of feminine noun, with its telltale *-ah* ending. These kinds of nouns, the *feminine* nouns, are almost always mirrors of abstract ideas in Hebrew, and so it is here: *qadmah* means "antiquity" or "a former state," the sort of thing one nostalgizes in retrospect, I suppose. So the Hebrews' antiquity, very much like their nostalgia, lay well to the east—where Paradise itself was, the proverbial and originary garden.

The paradox in this Hebraic conception of Paradise is that it was a garden that was actually no garden at all—because no one worked it, and because no one really worked at all. Here is how one superb gardening writer, Jim Nollman, understands this elusive relationship between ancient fantasy gardens and conceptions of paradise: "Paradise is elusive, which may explain why this writing about paradise tends to wander about its central premise as much as I wander about my garden. . . . Everything Adam and Eve ever needed was right there for the taking. The oldest profession was foraging."[15] Gardens and Paradise: what if they are not the same thing at all? Foraging, after all, has little to do with gardening. Maybe, just maybe, the ancient Hebrews weren't nearly as nostalgic as we tend to assume too quickly that they were. Maybe our notion of Paradise doesn't need to claim some cataclysmic loss or crisis as the human birthright. Maybe that is a Christian interpretive excess, born of a fundamental misunderstanding of gardens, then converted into something called "original sin." The Hebrews' initial conception of paradise was not exactly a garden; it was a place for foraging, and for gathering. What if the ancient Hebrews, who thought a great deal about gardens and cultivation, really had their sights trained on a *new* place, a *western* place, a place in which they might actually garden on their own?

If you take all of the early gardening images in the Book seriously, as I do, then they bear some startling implications. The only gardener in Eden is God. Adam and the Woman eat without toiling. They are literally pests, pests which God chooses to tolerate. ("What is a weed?" asks Emerson in a related vein. "A plant whose virtues have not yet been dis-

---

14. This is how the root appears in Gen 2:14, where the four rivers flowing out of the Garden of Eden are described, and the third of them, the Tigris, is said to flow *qidmath, to the east* of Assyria.

15. Nollman, *Why We Garden*, 55.

covered"). For the Couple to become, well, *human*, and not merely pests in God's paradise, they may well need to find a garden of their own to labor in, so that their virtues may be unlatched. Later rabbis were to ponder and develop these shocking possibilities, suggesting that the leisure and largesse of Eden is precisely what got the primordial couple into trouble in the first place. They simply had too much free time. Human beings *need* to labor, largely on their own.

This becomes a matter of great importance later on, if for no other reason than that the way any story begins so clearly effects the way it ends. If the human story began in a Garden, and if God works in a circle, then we may expect to end up in a garden, too, if we are lucky. It's always fascinating when Heaven is conceived as a garden, as a sort of Paradise regained. That is how the Qur'an seems to envision it: "God has promised the men and women who believe in Him gardens watered by running streams, in which they shall abide for ever: goodly mansions in the gardens of Eden."[16] That same image, of the Garden regained, recurs many times.[17] But that is a significantly later re-telling; I am not so sure that Genesis reads quite that way, and neither were the rabbis. If human beings were not originally gardeners, but rather foragers and pests... and if God works in a wavy line rather than a circle . . . well then. Then maybe we need to look *elsewhere* for a homecoming. I will return to that idea when we take a closer look at "the Fall" that comes so soon and so sadly into this story.

As is probably clear by now, I normally spend my days reading and writing and thinking about *Greek* stories, not Hebrew or Arabic ones. Three reasons occur to me as partial explanations of that professional preference. Of course, I fell in love with Homer as a child, and that may have been the end of the matter right there. But I'm looking for more by way of fully explaining this. Why this love-affair with Greek? First, there does seem to be a lingering Christian bias in our not-so-secular culture, a culture that contributed to my own cultivation, and that seems still to favor the "new" testament over the "old" one.[18] That new "testament" was written in Greek, not Hebrew, and Christians are always in danger of forgetting their Greek roots, whenever they emphasize their Jewish

---

16. Qur'an 9:72.

17. Qur'an 13:20–24, 16:31, 18:30–31, 19:60, 35:34, 38:50–51, 61:12.

18. Really, the Greek word, *diathêkê*, means a "covenant" rather than a "testament," and refers to the all-important Hebrew conception of a *b'rith*.

ones to Greek exclusion.[19] Christianity is the product of an original art of religious grafting; it's easy to forget that. Secondly, there seems to me to be an undeniably *pagan* element in our culture as well, one which derives from another significant feature of modern culture: Romanticism.[20] That "pagan" influence, which had already left a lasting imprint on the New Testament and on early Christian culture, lingers still in the long-lived fascination with Greek things in "western" cultures today. Third and finally, I see great significance in the fact that I garden "in the South," where both of these cultural influences converge in a confusing, and to me highly moving, mish-mash of Greek Stoicism and Christianity.[21]

Whatever the reasons, then—and they *are* various—I normally spend my days reading Greek stories rather than Hebrew ones. And whatever its source, I was startled with a singular feeling of smiling recognition when I came upon this strange Semitic verbal root (*q-d-m*) and its suggestive range of semantic meanings—from geography, through antipathy, to nostalgia. For *Cadmus*, that curious figure from the subtle *pre*history of Greek mythology, also hailed "from the east." His name seems to derive, in fact, from this selfsame Semitic root.[22] Just as the early Frankish Crusaders called their Muslim counterparts "Saracens," deriving the name from the Arabs' own word for "the east" (*sharc*), so the Greeks presumably named this weird and highly influential eastern figure in his own barbaric tongue. Q-D-M. Add a good Greek ending (-OS) to this Semitic root, and you've pretty well got his name: Qadamos.

Cadmus. One of the oddest figures in the rogue's gallery of Greek mythology. And I can think of no better guide to this rogue, or to that gallery, than a remarkable book written several years ago by an Italian

---

19. This was the actual topic Pope Benedict XVI addressed in his now notorious Regensburg lecture, with its bizarre Byzantine story about "Persian" intolerance. *Christian anti-Hellenism* was the Pope's real worry; and he thinks both the Protestant Reformation and Modernism contributed to its contemporary prominence. The text of that speech is available at http://www.cwnews.com/news/viewstory.cfm?recnum=46474

20. The Canadian philosopher, Charles Taylor, in his masterful *Sources of the Self*, esp. 305–493, paints a lovely picture of the influence of various European Romanticisms on the nineteenth century, as well as their lingering "aftermath" today in North America.

21. Walker Percy has written a wonderful essay analyzing just this strange southern concoction; it's called "Stoicism in the South," and appears in a posthumous volume entitled *Signposts in a Strange Land*, 83–88. I played with these ideas in a different register in my "The South as Tragic Landscape."

22. Morris, *Daidalos and the Origins of Greek Art*, 153.

publisher named Roberto Calasso. This sort-of mythical encyclopedia, sort-of modern novel, sort-of classical compendium is called *The Marriage of Cadmus and Harmony*, and it's got an entire chapter[23] devoted to its titular figurehead. I am indebted to this book for any sense I have been able to make of this mysterious figure and his rather unusual traveler's career.

For Cadmus was a wanderer, in every sense. Technically speaking, he was Phoenician, whatever that meant to people at the time.[24] Whatever else it meant, Cadmus's Phoenician identity suggests to us that he was a trader, a member of what was perhaps the first "transnational community" of the eastern Mediterranean. The Greeks were the second. My dear friend, Artemis Leontis, has written a marvelous essay in which she applies this same idea to the modern Greek identity, emphasizing the constitutive role of commerce (*emporion*) in this ethnic dispersion.[25] It's an old story: Greeks travel all over the world, opening restaurants, florist shops, and supermarkets. They work really hard for some decades, then go home, if they are so fortunate. The "Phoenicians," long before the "Greeks," conceived of themselves as a maritime culture, a culture-on-the-move, an emphatically mercantile, trading culture, and thus a culture that could be exported. Phoenicians apparently set themselves up in port colonies all over the eastern Mediterranean. According to Hegel, they even exited the straits of Gibraltar and were thus the first Mediterranean peoples to explore the open Atlantic.

> The Phoenicians discovered and first navigated the Atlantic Ocean. They had settlements in Cyprus and Crete. In the remote island of Thasos, they worked gold mines. In the south and southwest of Spain they opened silver mines. In Africa they founded the colonies of Utica and Carthage. From Gades they sailed far down the African coast, and according to some, even circumnavigated Africa. From Britain they brought tin, and from the Baltic, Prussian amber. This opens up an entirely new principle. Inactivity ceases, as also mere rude valor; in their place appears the activity

---

23. Calasso, *Marriage of Cadmus and Harmony*, 377–91.

24. The wonderful anthology edited by Sabatino Moscati, *Phoenicians*, provides a good place to start in attempting an answer to that question.

25. The essay is called "Mediterranean Topographies Before Balkanization: On Greek Diaspora, *Emporion*, and Revolution."

> of Industry, and that considerate courage which, while it dares the perils of the deep, rationally bethinks itself of the means of safety.... Human will and activity here occupy the foreground, not Nature and its bounty.... The sailor relies upon himself amid the fluctuation of the waves, and eye and heart must be always open.... Intelligence is the valor needed here, and ingenuity is better than natural courage.[26]

These are lecture notes, pithy and summary by design, but Hegel is onto something here, I think. He begins by noticing that not every culture imagines itself on the move this way, and then he attends to what the Greeks called "nature and culture," the way human artfulness transforms the natural world and gets commerce moving. These are the keys: commerce and industry, high courage and daring, cunning intelligence—these virtues of Odysseus are actually Phoenician in inspiration, Hegel suggests. So Cadmus would have had them, first.

His mythography, in any event, takes us back to the very beginning of things, back to when gods and mortals interacted far more closely than they ever do now. Cadmus's grandmother was Io. She was kidnaped and raped by Zeus, then metamorphosed by the jealousy of Hera, wandering the earth—always it is the *wandering* that strikes us in these stories—in the form of a heifer. Cadmus's sister was Europa, also kidnaped by Zeus, in the form of a bull this time, then taken *across the sea* and ravished in vast, Olympian ecstasy. Cadmus's father, a King called Agenor, ordered his four sons to set out in search of their lost sister, but only Cadmus steered a straight course. The other brothers abandoned their search, and so disappear from our story. Cadmus, by contrast, was diverted only once—just long enough to save Zeus, and the entire Olympian order, from the semi-successful attack of a monster called Typhon. Through Cadmus's cleverness, Zeus retrieves his severed tendons, and his stolen thunderbolts, then buries the would-be conqueror of the gods beneath the smoking peak of Mount Etna, in Sicily. Cadmus is promised Harmony—the surpassingly beautiful love-child of Aphrodite and Ares—as his reward.

And so Cadmus happens upon the rocky coast of Samothrace, in the northern Aegean, sailing west from home. He is feasted and feted, then finally given Harmony (such a pretty thing to be able to say!), at the gods' insistence. The girl eventually agrees to the match, after some se-

26. Hegel, *Philosophy of History*, 191–92.

ductive coaching from her servants. Then the couple sets off to complete Cadmus's search for his own wide-wandering sister, until the god himself orders the couple to give up their quest. At Delphi, Cadmus is informed that he will never find what he is looking for (does this mean his sister? we wonder... or happiness, and a home?). Instead, Apollo orders Cadmus to do three things, things that resonate powerfully and will find their echo in the Hebrew Bible. First and foremost, he is ordered to leave his home and his father behind, to think no more of Tyre, where they used to live, nor of nearby Sidon, where his sister was stolen away. Presumably, Cadmus is to think no more of his own people, either. He is ordered to settle *in the west*, and to found a *new* city, in the general neighborhood of Delphi, on the northern Greek mainland. And he is ordered to name this city "Thebes," after the Egyptian city with which he also has a mysterious, and as yet undefined, connection. Cadmus obeys. Cadmus always obeys.

He founds the city, building it on a massive scale. It is a walled city, with proud ramparts and seven famously fortified gates. The first festival in the city's history is the long-awaited marriage of Cadmus and Harmony, to which all of the Olympians are invited, and which they all joyfully attend, bearing such gifts as are appropriate to their station, and their unwitting savior. The couple—happy or no, it's never entirely clear—have four daughters: Autonoë, Ino, Agave and Semele. The latter two are the most meaningful, from the point of view of myth-making. Semele, of course, enjoyed Zeus's sexual favors, as so many of her forebears had done. But she made the mistake of demanding that she see her lover "face to face" (he only came to her at night, veiled in an obscure Olympian darkness). So Zeus came to her as a thunderbolt, and his shattering presence killed her where she stood. But Zeus saved the child she was carrying. And that child is Dionysus. Once grown, this newborn, latterly Olympian would travel west to Cadmus's city, demanding recognition and worship there. When the boy-king, Pentheus, resists this new marauder-god, he is murdered by his own mother, Agave, who is inspired—or maddened, depending on your point of view—by his cousin, the god himself. The justice of the gods being what it is—or isn't—Cadmus and Harmony are ordered to leave the city, to pursue their exile even further to the west, in Illyria. Cadmus left only one thing behind,[27] in addition to the smok-

---

27. Or possibly two things, if you believe a later Roman tradition that insisted

ing wreckage of the city he had built. Cadmus, who was a Phoenician, brought the technology of the written word with him from the east. And in teaching it to the Greeks, he unwittingly gave them an entirely new way to conceptualize, to love, and to honor their gods. Once they'd added the vowels . . .

Now this, I know, is a *very* strange sequence of stories. A mysteriously "eastern" figure is ordered to travel to the west by a god. He obeys. He always obeys. He leaves all thought of father and family behind, founds a new city, and succeeds in every significant task to which he turns (save the original one of locating his long-suffering sister). Eventually, new troubles will engage his immediate relations, and all of his descendants; he will be forced into further wanderings, and a definitive final exile. Cadmus settles in the west, and his people will eventually define the cultural identity of that foreign, adoptive place. This constitutes a pattern we will meet again, with Abraham. But the emphasis on *writing* is unique to Cadmus, that magical technology of curious scribal marks. Abraham does not write, and so he had no scripture, as we have seen. This appears to be a highly significant, and eminently Greek, detail. It helps to make the novel notion of bittersweet, erotic love possible, a concept we will not be able to dig up in the Hebrew Book at all.

Now, in this book of mine, I am leaving the Greeks behind—or rather, I am wandering away from my adoptive literary homeland, to bring it into conversation, and even into translation, with other places and other times. If the ancient Greeks were not simply "pagans". . . and if the ancient Hebrews were not simply "monotheists". . . and if their stories often overlap in curious and intriguing ways . . . well then, they may have a lot to learn from one another, *if* we bring their stories into conversation. That is what I propose to do here. But to do this work well, I think we need to work a bit harder to hear the Greeks, lest the more bombastic "monotheists" to whom we uncritically grant religious precedence drown their voices out.

I want to spend some time meditating on the unusual semantic range of this *Hebrew* root, Q-D-M, a complex of words that signifies everything from the eastern quarter of the compass to a cosmic place of meeting. I want to think about what the resonances of this "eastern-ness" were

---

Cadmus was a fine cook as well. This may be found in Athenaeus's marvelous compendium, *Deipnosophistes* ("Scholars at Supper") 14.658ff.

in the Hebrew Bible, specifically in the weirdly compelling first twenty-five chapters of the book of Genesis. Admittedly, even the book-title is Greek, not Hebrew. Characteristically, the first five books of the Hebrew Bible are named after the first word in each one. So the (Greek) book of Genesis, in Hebrew, is referred to simply as *b'reshit*, "in the beginning." For my purposes, however, I will refer to the book as "Genesis," which is what it became when certain talented, if largely anonymous, scholars in Egyptian Alexandria translated their holy scripture into (what else?) the Greek language, vowels and all.

The legends concerning the creation of the Septuagint expanded and changed considerably through time. And since the Septuagint served more as a Christian than a Jewish Bible, Jews and Christians remembered this story very differently.[28] The story begins when the Head Librarian in Alexandria convinced his emperor to acquire the sacred scriptures of other peoples, including those of the Jews. Antiochus sent an embassy to Jerusalem, received the texts in Hebrew but couldn't read them, so he pled for a Greek translation in addition. A group of seventy-two scholars (later reduced to seventy in the myth, hence the name *Sept*uagint) traveled to Alexandria, roughed out their translation, then were sent home with astonishing gifts for their Temple (and for their trouble). Later Christians emphasized the *miraculous* quality of the event, claiming that each man worked alone (or else in teams of two) and that they all created identical versions with divine guidance. Later rabbis drew up lists of the thirteen (or more) passages that were changed by this shift from Hebrew to Greek ... and worried about the *distortions*. Indeed, we now know that there were many translations of the Bible in circulation, more than one Septuagint.[29] These worries aside, I will consult both versions of Genesis, the Hebrew original and the Greek translation, as I proceed with the process of trying to make my own.

While what I am doing is sketchy and incomplete—little more than the plowing before seedtime, which will need to wait on some other, later project—I want to focus on the two biblical characters who frame these essential introductory chapters: Adam and Abraham. The one encom-

---

28. For more on that legend, see Wasserstein and Wasserstein, *Legend of the Septuagint*, which traces this primordial urban legend from the Hellenistic world to today.

29. The version I am using was edited by a remarkable German scholar named Alfred Rahlfs, who inherited the project at the end of the First World War, but did not complete it until 1935, when the times, and his own country, had decidedly changed.

passes a story of gardening (or foraging), of rootedness to place—at least in the beginning. The other embodies a story of migration, uprooting, nearly continual displacement. Between these two characters, and their interwoven sets of stories, a complex view of the human world begins to emerge.

I begin, then, with the first time the Hebrew root (q-d-m) appears—specifically, in a garden, a garden called "Eden." The name seems to suggest some sort of very *earthy* pleasure. For starters, I want to pay attention to what the Hebrew looks like. Woefully inadequate as my own Hebrew is (I studied it a *very* long time ago, while I was still in graduate school), I will nonetheless try to consult the Hebrew in the Book, and not merely the Greek of the Septuagint, or the English authorized by King James.[30] I will not use any of the elaborate critical apparatuses of the scholars here, and any textual comments or discussion worth having about specific passages will appear in the body of my book. I am not writing a piece of biblical criticism after all, not really. What I am doing is attempting to render the sounds of Hebrew into a kind of Anglo-American; my practice here is not standard and is, from the scholarly point-of-view, probably pretty substandard. So, with all these disclaimers suitably in place, here we go. The passage is Genesis 2:8, and I'll look at it first in Hebrew:

> wayyitta' YHWH Elohim gan-b'Eden *miqqedem* vayyasem sham et-ha'adam asher yatzar.

Next I look at the Greek:

> kai ephyteusen kyrios ho theos paradeison en Edem *kata anatolas* kai etheto ekei ton anthrôpon, hon eplasen.

And now we come to the English translation of this highly regarded and well-known biblical verse, but one which is not mine. The English version of Genesis that I have elected to use in this book comes from a marvelous translation by Everett Fox, entitled *The Five Books of Moses*. Influenced by the profound meditations on biblical translation of several famous early twentieth-century Jewish scholars (like Franz Rosenzweig, Martin Buber, and Walter Benjamin), the stop-start, think-and-mull-it-over quality of Fox's translation fits very nicely with what I am trying to

---

30. In so doing, I am using the famous 1977 scholarly edition, the *Biblia Hebraica Stuttgartensia*.

do. Moreover, Everett Fox consistently includes, wherever possible, the meaning of place-names and personal names that were clearly intended to mean something, in Hebrew. He marks them that way with a slash in the text. So here, the Hebrew, *gan-b'Eden*, becomes "a garden in Eden/Land of Pleasure" in English. Like so many other things in his weird-but-wonderful translation, once I had accustomed myself to his stylistic practices, I found myself enjoying and appreciating its style, and its own unique rhythms, very much. Fox helped me to enter into what must be confessed to be a very foreign, ancient Hebrew brainscape. Here is how he puts the passage before us:

> YHWH, God, planted a garden in Eden/Land-of-Pleasure, *in the east*,
> and there he placed the human whom he had formed.

Maybe you are beginning to see my question now, my first point of entry into this strange story. God first gardened *miqqedem*, "in the east." East, I began to wonder, of *where*?

chapter three

EAST

Why is He said to have planted Paradise in Eden toward the East?

In the first place, because the movement of the world is from East to West; and that from which movement starts is first. Second, that which is in the region of the East is said to be the right side of the world, while that in the region of the West is the left. And so [Homer] testifies, calling the birds in the region of the East "right," and those which are in the region of the West "on the left side." If they go to the right side, it is to the day and the sun; but if to the left, toward evening and darkness. But the name Eden when translated is certainly a symbol of delicacies, joy and mirth. For all good things have their origin in this sacred place.[1]

...

But to the place where, it standeth north-north-east and by east from the west corner of thy curious-knotted garden....[2]

...

My garden faces to the east, in a curious way. Squarish gardens like mine have four sides, I know, so technically speaking, they face all four corners

---

1. Philo *Questions and Answers on Genesis* 1.7.
2. Shakespeare, *Love's Labour's Lost*, 1.1.

of the compass. As do empires. But it's a more complex matter of *orientation* I'm after, here. So is the Book, I have come to believe.

I am preoccupied by that idea as I walk the slow perimeter this morning—cradling my coffee cup, moving slowly now from sun to shadow to sun again—intrigued by how unconscious I was of such matters when first I laid out the lines of my own garden. I did not think about what I was doing very well. And that serene lack of self-consciousness did not seem to do me any great harm. I was careful to position the garden in as open a space as I could manage, and as far from the encroaching shade of the largish trees that line this property. But what interests me now is how naturally my body—and, by curious extension, my garden as well—was oriented toward the east, which is to say, oriented toward the morning sun in springtime. Almost without thinking, I laid out my garden facing to the east. And so, as the Book makes a point of reiterating several times, did God. The primordial Paradise garden apparently faced east. Now there is a rich gardener's tradition—one which extends from the old Roman, Pliny the Elder (23–79 CE), to the Renaissance architect, Leon Battista Alberti (1404–1472 CE)—one that notes that gardens should ideally face "south," not east. (Poor Alberti. Even his biographer, Giorgio Vasari, notes that his *writings* were worth much more than his *art*. Vasari should know; people said the same thing about him). Of course, in our vastly more global era, we'd do better to say that gardens should face toward the equator—facing south if you're gardening in Europe or North America, but you'd actually need to face north if you were in Australia, say, or Kenya. Still, such borders are blurry; east and south blur into one another here, metamorphosing along with the sun's sensual, seasonal flip-flops. The summer solstice is among the most magical of days, to the gardener—that magical evening luster, and long, lingering light. In hot places such as Atlanta—or Athens, or Rome—*shade* management may become nearly as important as the sun. Light and darkness demand a balance. "A southern exposure" may be the ideal, but if you *live* in the south, closer to the equator, then you're likely to be more focused on the east—as the Book is.

Many have remarked upon the curious narrative "frame" that surrounds this biblical garden. In front of it looms the massive trauma of Creation itself, day after shattering day of it. Immediately after it comes the Fall, the colossal fracture between the human and divine realms, all of this requiring a single day, a single extended narrative moment, as it were. But between Creation and the Fall, there is a Garden.

There is a poetry in naming, as few literatures attest more eloquently than the Hebrew Bible. "A word is no light matter," says Edith Hamilton. "Words have with truth been called fossil poetry, each, that is, a symbol of creative thought."[3] "Genesis," as I indicated, is the *Greek* name for this eminently Hebraic idea: the sudden and fairly spontaneous creation of everything that exists, day piled upon creative day, through the active agency of a single God, and the naming of each and every element in it as "good." Genesis is like springtime, the very birthday of the world. Then the evil comes.

This garden of mine looks to the east, and very much like Eden in the Book, it blossoms explosively in the springtime then spills brilliantly over its borders in the summer. But there is a problem with the parallel I'm attempting to draw. There is not one record of creation, so there's no singular picture of that pleasure-garden. Many biblical scholars, especially the so-called source critics who make so much of the textual "seams" I will also be trying to notice, have commented on the implicit picture of the world we are getting in this biblical account of divine Creation.[4] I said "biblical account of Creation," but it would be more accurate to refer to the plural *accounts* of the biblical Creation, for there are two of them, not one, and they are joined at a subtle textual seam we can still just barely make out at Genesis 2:4, when the story begins anew. In fact, the Septuagint marks this seam very clearly, by adding a summary phrase that seems almost like a title-piece: "This is the book of the generations of the heaven and the earth. On the day when God . . ."

The rabbis who first noticed this scriptural seam also noticed how *wet* things seem in the first account:

> when the earth was wild and waste,
> darkness over the face of Ocean,
> rushing-spirit of God hovering over the face of the waters—
> God said:

---

3. Hamilton, *The Greek Way*, 230.

4. I owe a great debt to Robert Graves and Raphael Patai, whose *Hebrew Myths*, especially 21–28, offers a treasure-trove of such scholarly and spiritual speculation.

> Let there be a dome amid the waters,
> and let it separate waters from waters!
> God made the dome
> and separated the waters that were below the dome from the waters that were above the dome.
> It was so.
> God called the dome: Heaven!
> There was setting, there was dawning: second day.[5]

God's hands seem filled with the overwhelming task of simply separating these waters of primordial chaos, and shoring up some solid ground on which to create a host of other things—birds of the air, beasts of the field, what have you. It looks and feels like a Mesopotamian world, the rabbis suggested, wet and loamy and wildly abundant. Scholars notice that this description also looks very similar to a Babylonian account of the creation of the world, similar in its way to what we find in a fascinating collection of seven cuneiform tablets called the *Enuma Elish*. The idea was that the rabbis probably learned these stories during their own Babylonian Captivity in the mid-500s BCE, then wrote them down when they returned home in the next generation. If Jerusalem is your implicit frame of reference for this story, and if you live in Babylon or Baghdad, then it looks for all the world as if the story has moved north, and "east."

Not so in the second creation account, the account that zeroes in on the *human* dimension of this divine drama. Here things seem, well, for starters they seem much *drier*.

> At the time of YHWH, God's making of earth and heaven,
> no bush of the field was yet on earth,
> no plant of the field had yet sprung up,
> for YHWH, God, had not made it rain upon earth,
> and there was no human/*adam* to till the soil/*adama*.[6]

There is clay, to be sure, but this clay is dry enough for God to form it into the shape of *ha'adam*, the man. And that clay then needs to have the breath of life—a wet, hot breath—breathed into it before it can claim to live at all. We really do seem to be on simpler, firmer, drier ground. We are decidedly nearer to the desert, decidedly further from the moistness

---

5. Gen 1:2, 6–8.
6. Gen 2:4–5.

of Mesopotamia. We are, as many have noticed, closer to a description of the land of Canaan. So it is not at all surprising that, when God elects to garden, God does so in the east, in what the biblical text specifically tells us is well-watered, eastern ground. But the man was not made there; he was brought there, the Book tells us, "to work it and to watch it,"[7] a point that is emphasized in this second account of Creation, but not the first one. Earlier, Adam and the Woman seemed to be desert foragers primarily. Is Adam a tenant farmer now, one designed by God to *work* this land? Or is he merely the blessed recipient of God's, and Eden's, impossible bounty? Does Adam work this land, or simply prosper on it? This is far more than an ecological question; it cuts to the very heart of the biblical conception of people and their purpose.

So, we have a sort of doubled Creation-account here, with one important geographical nuance and a lingering cartographic question: *Where are we?* In the irrigated fields of Mesopotamia? Or in the desert wastes of Canaan? Interesting as that question is—and my earlier pondering about the "eastern-ness" of the description makes it decisive—equally interesting is the question of *when*? *When did this Creation take place?* Is it autumn, or springtime? The rabbis have argued for millennia over this question.

Those more assimilated Jewish thinkers—by which I mean the ones assimilated to the Greco-Romanized culture of the age (and therefore much more popular among Christians than their Jewish brethren, as I have already said)—men such as Philo of Alexandria (ca. 20 BCE–50 CE), whom we met at the beginning of this chapter, argued that the universe had been created in the springtime. In fact, Philo even suggested that the "doubled" account of this Creation may well have had a Platonic reason: God first created bodiless (*asômata*) forms of things, *Platonic* forms, and then later created the material things themselves.[8]

There is an interesting logic to this springtime view, one laid out very clearly by Philo himself. In dialogue with the older Greek philosophers who worried about such things—namely, about whether or not the cosmos could really be eternal—Philo assumes that either: (a) the universe experienced no "Creation," has no beginning and no end, and thus it is eternal; or (b) it had a clear beginning and will have an equally

---

7. Gen 2:15.

8. He develops this idea in his *Questions and Answers on Genesis* 1.19, a book to which I will return below.

dramatic end; or else (c) the universe as we know it had a sudden beginning, its Creation by God, but it will *never* have an end. Philo himself inclines to this third view (he discusses it in great detail in an essay entitled "On the Eternity of the World"), and significantly enough, he locates the beginning of it all in the springtime. Spring, after all, is when *most* natural things begin, or rather, when they begin again—some Greek and Roman Stoics were tempted to believe that repeated conflagrations had periodically destroyed the worlds with fire (Cadmus would not have been surprised). Other rabbis, beginning with the Rabbi Eliezer, whose career flourished around 90 CE, argued for an autumnal Creation, and their views gradually triumphed, at least among the orthodox. I'll return to that point below. As I have meditated on these texts, it looks to me as if the *first* Creation account took place in the springtime, whereas the second one looks for all the world like the fall. One account seems vaguely "pagan," indebted to Mesopotamian and Babylonian models, while the other seems more authentically Judean, more homegrown. So, which one to choose?

These are modern, scholarly preoccupations, in the main. They are the product of a fairly modern way of looking at biblical texts, analyzing them with an eye to their prior sources, their compositional histories, and to be sure, their textual variations. Biblical scholars in the nineteenth century, especially in German-speaking university-cultures, took to the Book with an impressive array of scholarly tools and methods. They seemed, at times, to be more interested in tearing the Book apart than in keeping it whole. They saw themselves as gardeners, turning over the rich biblical soil, to air it out, but others saw them as bandits, thieves, or worse. That is one reason why a group of anti-modern Christians who began calling themselves "fundamentalists" in the 1920s, right here in the U.S., rejected all of these "modern" methods of biblical dissection, and the "liberal" theology on which it was based. Fundamentalism—then as now, Christian and otherwise—knew who its enemy was, and knew what it was fighting: liberalism, modernity, an age of alleged fragmentation and disbelief. Or so they said. And still say, whether they are Jewish, Christian, or Muslim.[9]

But it was never an entirely fair criticism. At the very least, it depended on a caricature of what those poor German professors and Greek

---

9. My dear friend, Bruce B. Lawrence, performed the first *comparative* study of such anti-modern religious movements in a wonderful and important book entitled *Defenders of God*.

philologists were really up to. Few of them were really motivated by an anti-Christian desire to pull the Book apart, nor by the atheistic desire to shake the foundations of the Christian faith. In many cases, their desires were just the opposite. Initially, they were, many of them at any rate, every bit as Romantic as the Fundamentalists who opposed them. While it may seem odd to many of us today, this careful poking and prodding at the Book, all of this scholarly collating of its various manuscript traditions and rescencions and redactions, all of this had one ultimate aim: *the Romantic quest for origins*. Many of these scholars believed—and they applied these same methods to the Homeric poems—that, by paring away all of the later scribal accretions, we might actually get back to the *original* book, something a bit closer to what Moses, or Homer, actually wrote. It was all part of a grand intellectual and spiritual project, a fabulous journey back to beginnings—the beginning of the Book, the beginning of humanity, the beginning of time.

This was also a theatrically and elaborately *Protestant* gesture, by and large. Once Martin Luther (1483–1546) and company had opened the floodgates, by calling for the *private* reading and *personal* study of the biblical texts, texts they translated into the vernacular languages, then a new spirit of critical engagement with the scriptures gradually ensued. Everyone had the right, and the duty, to read the Book—*on their own*. Protestantism was thus clearly motivated by this same general quest: the quest for Christian origins. The idea was to get back to *original* Christianity, and back to its originary right-relation with God. Paul was rediscovered; so was Paul's version of Adam and of Eden, and Augustine's version of sin and the fall. Abraham was rediscovered too, if a bit more obliquely. I'll return to that issue later on.

One of the most fascinating early modern representatives of such an approach was James Ussher (or Usher, 1581–1656), a prominent Protestant professor from Dublin and later the archbishop of Armagh. His parents were both Protestants at a time when this was relatively new. (Curiously though, Ussher's mother converted to Catholicism shortly before her death. What mark this left on the son we can only speculate). The son was enrolled at Trinity College, Dublin, which was also very new. In fact, he was enrolled at the ripe young age of thirteen, in the very year the College first opened its doors. He was a voracious reader, a prodigious bibliophile, equally gifted in all the ancient languages (Hebrew, Greek, and Latin) and in ancient histories and chronologies. He taught as a professor at Trinity College for many years, until he took up the ecclesial

James Ussher (1581–1656)

office in 1620, having devoted his entire career to the close study of classical and biblical literature, as well as that vast corpus of early Christian writings we call "patristics." He applied all of these ancient materials to modern problems—specifically, to ongoing religious disputes within the Anglican fold. Rabidly anti-Catholic, a royalist defender of the divine rights of monarchy, the Bishop Ussher was also renowned as one of the most learned religious minds of his age.

He wrote an enormous amount, but of special interest to me is a quirky, longish book that was written just two years prior to his death, in 1654. It is generally known as *The Annals of the World*, and in fact, the Emory University Library where I was permitted to look over a rare copy of this handsome folio edition, has it listed in the catalogue with precisely that title. But the Bishop's title page bears a longer, and more interesting, title:

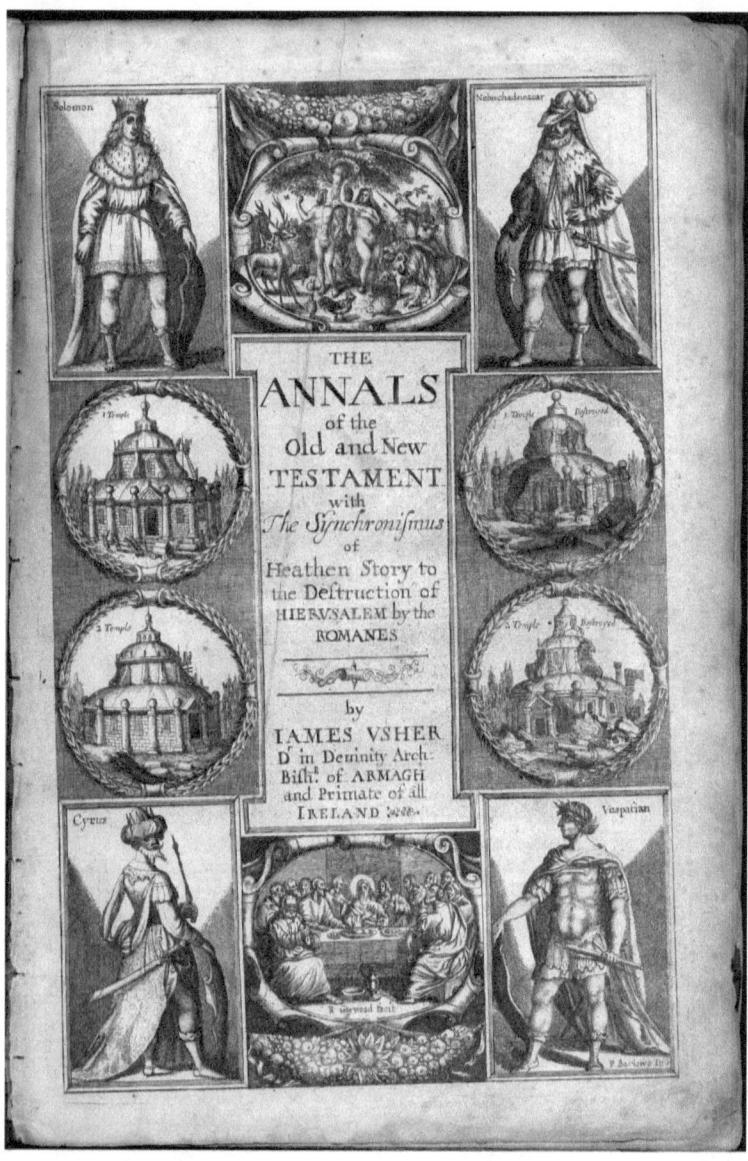

Illustrated title page from Ussher's *Annals of the World*

The full text on the very next page is also highly illuminating, and fascinating for the historical and cultural nuances it provides:

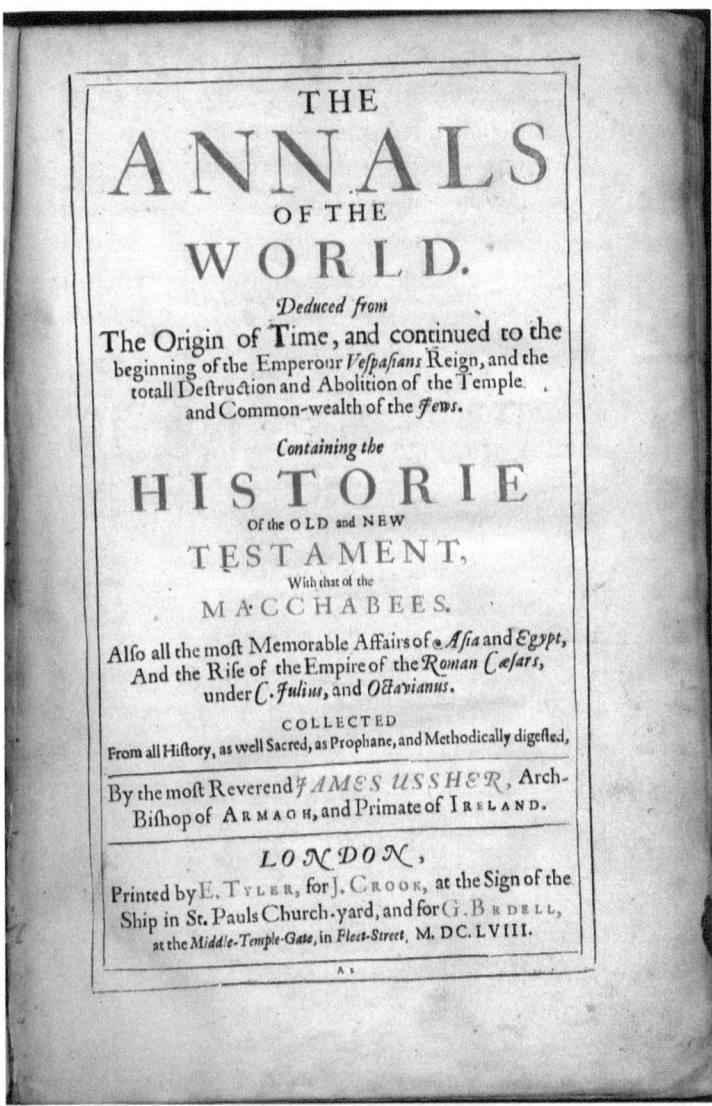

Full-text title page from *Annals of the World*

Bishop Ussher's book was conceived as an elaborate attempt to bring all the major pagan sources—Egyptian and Chaldean histories, astronomical calculations, Greek and Roman historiography, etcetera—into dialogue with the more orthodox Hebrew and early Christian chronicles. He is *blending* the "sacred" and the "profane" in a way that was destined to make us all modern. But whereas most pagan philosophers had despaired of ever discovering the exact time and date of cosmic creation (still others did not believe that there *was* a date, since the world has always been, eternally), and whereas later Christian humorists like Mark Twain cut elegantly through the Gordian knot of such disputations by assuming that the world was simply created on the first of January,[10] James Ussher proudly noted that the modern, Protestant literary "sciences" were the first[11] to have finally and conclusively resolved the mystery. Here is how he explains his reasoning. He begins, tellingly enough, with the death of a *pagan* emperor, King Nebuchadnezzar, whose presence in the biblical texts[12] may now be cross-referenced to his place in more local, Chaldean histories:

> [Nebuchadnezzar's death] fell out in the 3442 year of the World, but by collation of Chaldean History, and the Astronomical Cannon, it fell out in the 186 year of Nabonasar, and, as by certain connexion, it must follow in the 562 year before the Christian account, and of the Julian Period, the 4152, and from thence I gathered the Creation of the World did fall out upon the 710 year of the Julian Period, *by placing its beginning in Autumn*: but for as much as the first day of the World began with the evening of the first day of the week, *I have observed that the Sunday*, which in the year 710 aforesaid, *came nearest the Autumnal Æquinox*, by Astronomical Tables, . . . happened upon the 23 day of the Julian October; from thence concluded, that from the evening preceding, that first day of the Julian year, both the first day of the Creation, and the first motion of time are to be deduced.
>
> The difficulties of Chronologers, perplexed by that φιλονεικία, or love of contention, so termed by Basil, being at last over-passed, I encline to this opinion, that from the evening ushering in the

---

10. In his "Autobiography of Eve," published in *Letters from the Earth*, 42.

11. In this, he was overreaching. Origen (c. 184–c. 254 CE) and Eusebius (c. 260–339 CE) had introduced these very methods to the Church fairly early in the imperial city of Caesarea. For more on their groundbreaking achievements, see Grafton and Williams, *Christianity and the Transformation of the Book*, esp. 18.

It is interesting to note that they dated the Creation to the sixth millennium BCE, not the 4th, as Bishop Ussher did. Every age, it seems, wishes to delay its own ending.

12. 2 Kgs 24:1—25:22, and 2 Chr 36:6–7.

first day of the World, to that midnight which began the first day of the Christian æra, there was 4003 years, seventy dayes, and six temporarie howers; and that the true Nativity of our Saviour was full four years before the beginning of the vulgar Christian æra, as is demonstrable by the time of *Herods* death. For according to our account, the building of *Solomons* Temple was finished in the 3000 year of the World, and in the 4000 year of the World, the dayes being fulfilled, in which the Blessed Virgin, Mother of God, was to bring forth Christ himself, (of whom the Temple was a Type) was manifest in the flesh, and made his first appearance unto man: from whence four years being added to the Christian æra, and as many taken away from the years before it, instead of the Common and Vulgar, we shall obtein a true and natural Epocha of the Nativity of Christ.[13]

It is dizzying stuff, to be sure, a curious mingle-mangle of hard science, soft science, and artful theology. It is equally telling what the right reverend does not feel the need to cross-reference, or defend. He simply *assumes* that the Creation took place in the autumn—he always was a staunch defender of Orthodoxy—and he simply *assumes* that it took place on a Sunday, somewhere near the autumnal equinox (I've highlighted these assumptions in the quotation). He also insists that there must be smooth symmetries, say, between the creation of one Temple and another (images of the two Jerusalem temples grace that first title page, be sure to note). But the end of the matter for the Bishop of Armagh is plain: God "created the heavens and the earth" on October 23, 4004 BCE.

> In the beginning God created Heaven and Earth, *Gen. 1 v.1*. Which beginning of time, according to our Chronologie, fell upon the entrance of the night preceding the twenty third day of *Octob.* in the year of the Julian Calendar, 710.
>
> Upon the first day therefore of the world, or *Octob.* 23. being our Sunday, God, together with the highest Heaven, created the Angels. Then having finished, as it were, the roofe of this building, he fell in hand with the foundation of this wonderfull Fabrick of the World, he fashioned this lowermost Globe, consisting of the Deep, and of the Earth; all the Quire of Angels singing together,

---

13. Ussher, *Annals of the World*, "The Epistle to the Reader," A-7, italics mine. Notes omitted.

> and magnifying his name therefore. [*Job.* 38.*v.*7]. And when the Earth was void and without forme, and darknesse covered the face of the Deepe, on the very middle of the first day, the light was created; which God severing from the darknesse, called the one day, and the other night.[14]

Maybe I'm more Protestant-ly inclined than I realize (U.S. culture still is, in the main, since such things change at a glacial pace and with mighty slowness), but for reasons poetical as well as terrestrial, I have opted for the autumn in my ruminations as well. It just so happens that I am putting the finishing touches to this book in the fall. I like the pretty poetry implicit in making the Fall take place in fall, thereby planting God's Garden decisively *at the end* of summer's heat and abundant fruition. It takes place in a time for harvesting, *and* for planting afresh.

James Ussher dated God's Creation to the wee hours of October the 23rd. Content to be a little less precise than the Bishop, I also imagine Creation taking place in the fall. My reasons differ, though; they have more to do with poetry than astronomy, and I owe them to a poet. Just a half-generation *before* the Bishop's cosmic computations, John Donne preached a poet's sermon that puts the point beautifully. It was Christmas evening, and the year was 1624.

> God made sun and moon to distinguish seasons, and day and night, and we cannot have the fruits of the earth but in their seasons: But God hath made no decree to distinguish the seasons of his mercies; in paradise, the fruits were ripe, the first minute, *and in heaven it is alwaies Autumn,* his mercies are ever in their maturity.[15]

It probably takes a poet to see and say things this way, and far better the poet who has tended a garden him- or herself: "He brought light out of darkness, not out of a lesser light; He can bring thy Summer out of Winter, though thou have no Spring," Donne says. So the seasons blur and shift in Paradise. And *"in heaven it is alwaies Autumn"*—with all due apology to Philo and his friends.

---

14. Ussher, *Annals of the World,* "The Annals of the Old Testament," 1.
15. As quoted in Capon, *Genesis: The Movie,* 59–60, italics mine.

chapter four

LABOR

The Vézère River curves among limestone hills covered by forest. At its lower reaches, just before it flows into the Dordogne, a large number of caves inhabited by Paleolithic man were discovered. His skeleton, found in Cro-Magnon, resembles contemporary man's. The Cro-Magnon probably originated in Asia; his progression towards Europe started after the last glaciation some thirty or forty thousand years before Christ. He pitilessly exterminated the less advanced Neanderthal, usurping his caves and hunting grounds. Man was born under the star of Cain.[1]

...

The sun has still not managed to cut completely through the canopy of this morning's clouds. After hours of failing effort, it is nearly noon now. It is colder than it has been, as I said, and I notice the first flock of birds on the move, high overhead. Doubtless they have come from further north where, so I am told, autumn has arrived in force. These feathered flocks from the north are on the road, migrating (a concept that will occupy my attention a great deal directly), in search of warmer, greener pastures. An enormous gaggle of them stop here just long enough to poke around the neighboring fields, looking for seed, then to toss my fresh grass clippings over with the careless abandon that makes waking up so interesting in

1. Herbert, *Barbarian in the Garden*, 8–9.

the fall. And then, just as swiftly and with a lonely aerial drama, they are gone.

A more unusual event transpired just after the birds set off. I was standing in one of the first, and deepest, garden beds I ever dug here, surveying the result of some heavier weeding and soil-turning I'd done a few days previously. As if out of nowhere, two brilliant and brightly colored golden butterflies arrived, and began their lover's dance almost poetically inside and around one another. The pattern of this dance matched the delicate patterning of their wings, or so it seemed as I watched. They stayed at it for quite some time, in a perfectly choreographed ballet of endearment. Even the dog was stunned into silent reverie, head tilted and ears perked, motionless and silenced before this apparition of pure love. Then, just as suddenly, one of the pair darted off. I hesitated, then turned, but could not locate him. And when I returned my appreciative gaze to his loving companion, she had disappeared as well, evaporated into thin air, so it seemed. Without an earthbound trace.

Flowers bear an important place in any serious garden. They help to attract the mad cacophony of wildlife that hums almost continuously about this place, the frantic buzz of fertility, the sheer and ebullient excess of life's never-ending desire for itself. While there may be some truth to the old adage that "humans couple, whereas animals mate," it's rather hard not to personalize the process as you see it unfold in a garden of your own making. And flowers complicate the thing considerably. If you are paying attention, then there seem to be urgent love-matters afoot here, each and every day. And yet, more often than not for the would-be flower lovers, for the two ever to meet, they require the intervention and graceful dance of a third, be it bumblebee, butterfly, or breeze. All of this triangulation, and a happy ambiance of good luck besides.[2]

God hardly seems fair to Adam and the Woman. I know how odd this must sound to any believer in what Christians still refer to as "original sin." But that's a later theological conception that we can of course read back into these stories. Still, it takes great care and forethought. And we should at least recall that Jews and Muslims have other ways of read-

---

2. For a lovely, and eminently French, description of such love matters, see Jean-Pierre Otte's *Love in the Garden*.

ing into them, born of subtly different Godward inclinations. So, for that matter, did other Christians, apparently right from the start. When an enormous cache of so-called Gnostic gospels was discovered in the Egyptian desert near a place called Nag Hammadi, on Christmas Day in 1945, then a new and very different window was opened onto this mysterious ancient world, the chaotic era of Christian origins.³ We will soon see just how many different ways the rabbis and early Christians had of understanding Adam and the Woman—their relationship to one another, and to God, and especially their varying conceptions of the mechanics of their Fall. It had a lot to do with freedom and autonomy, and especially with taking responsibility, less to do directly with sex and desire and an ultimately uncontrollable human nature. That all came later.

In fact, it appears as if St. Augustine (354–430 CE, a Roman citizen who hailed from the north African coast, lived in Italy for a time, converted as an adult, then returned to north Africa for the remainder of his long life) managed a massive reinterpretation of the story told in Genesis chapter 3, one that, for all of its lyricism and philosophical artfulness, is anchored in a radical new theology of "original sin."⁴ It also appears as if his domineering rhetorical voice, with its overwhelming vision of an utterly corrupted human nature, gradually drowned out most of the others. In the west—wherever that is—we have learned to read this story much as Augustine did, and to see in it what he saw: namely, the shattering fact of human viciousness, its idolizing of its own autonomy, its fundamental rebellion against dependence on God. And in so doing, we forget the other stories, somehow fail to hear the other voices at all. Augustine did not know Islam, which had not happened yet, but the rabbinic discussions he might well have known.⁵

---

3. See Robinson, "Discovery of the Nag Hammadi Codices," as well as the complete translation of these documents available in Robinson, *Nag Hammadi Library*, and in an abbreviated form in Miller, *Complete Gospels*. Elaine Pagels was one of the first to interpret this material for a popular audience in *Gnostic Gospels*, though her views seem to have changed significantly in *Beyond Belief*.

The quote I use on the frontispiece is taken from one of these wisdom-seeking texts, preserved as "The Gospel of Philip."

4. A quite brilliant rumination on this theological quandary may be found in Rose Macauley's *Towers of Trebizond*, 229–33.

5. Pagels offers a wonderful summary of this complex material in *Adam, Eve and the Serpent*, especially pages 98–126, on these, Augustine's long-lived Genetic musings.

Certainly the justice of God is a very real, but also highly complex issue in this story. It is God who places the tree (or trees) in the garden in the first place, after all, as a sort of test that God should seem to know that this first couple was doomed to fail. Moreover, as Philo noted, the couple's morals were terribly simplistic at the time ("the most simplistic," he says, *dia tên tôn êthôn haplotêta*), and thus they were both easily misled.[6] Mark Twain developed that idea with scathing precision in many of his later writings, published and no, as we shall see. Lacking the knowledge of good and evil, it is hard to see how the first couple could conceive of wrongdoing, disobedience, or sin. Lacking any experience of death, it is harder still to imagine how they could possibly have conceived of the enormity of the stakes before them, the risks they were running, or the threat to their posterity.

In addition to all of this, a rabbinically trained Holocaust survivor, Elie Wiesel, makes much of what seems an eerily predestinarian dimension to this story, in his wonderful collection of biblical meditations and midrashic character-sketches, entitled *Messengers of God*. Wiesel even refers to one strange rabbinic tradition which seems to suggest that this primal act of human disobedience actually contributed to the fuller development of humanity, the actual *completion* of human (self)creation:

> [T]he first couple *had* to violate the divine commandment to allow mankind to evolve. Had Adam and Eve opted for life and against knowledge, history would have ended with them. There would have been no punishment, no death, no struggle for survival, no nothing, no nobody. Adam and Eve *had* to defy God so that their descendants might sing His praises. They were not free, hence not responsible. . . .
>
> According to Jewish tradition, creation did not end with man, it began with him. When He created man, God gave him a secret—*and that secret was not how to begin but how to begin again*.[7]

I once heard of a club created at a high school by some erstwhile, college-bound seniors. Inviting certain select juniors to join the club, they happened upon the perfect initiation rite. Each young man in turn was selected, interviewed, and then told to stand for fully five minutes in the

---

6. Philo *Questions and Answers on Genesis* 1.30.
7. Wiesel, *Messengers of God*, 27, 32; emphasis mine.

corner of the room—*without* thinking about a pink polar bear. No one who was honest ever joined the club. The Tree of the Knowing of Good and Evil just *is* that pink polar bear. Once its fruit was forbidden, it would be all the two humans could think about.

So there is a tree, and it is simply *there*. It is specifically set apart by God as taboo, as forbidden. No reasons are given; none, it seems, are needed. And yet it is primarily this *absence* of a reason, we may assume, that prompts the two humans to eat. Where, exactly, was the crime in that? Disobedience to a clear divine command is easy enough to see in this story, but it is harder to conceive for creatures who have no moral conception yet. And in any case, it is always harder for people to obey commands that seem to have no reason. God is surely a Father here, one who treats Adam and the Woman both as children; their act of primal defiance is also ironically an act of growing up—not merely of acting out. What is maturity, if it is not learning to see the answer "because I am your Father and I said so" as inadequate? Here is how Mark Twain envisioned this catastrophic Fall, as anticipated and understood by another fallen angel who witnessed it, if he did not actually coax it along. The fallen angel conducts the interview:

> "Well, obedience to constituted authority is a moral law. Suppose Adam should forbid you to put your child in the river and leave it there over night—would you put the child there?"
>
> She answered with a darling simplicity and guilelessness—
>
> "Why, yes, if I wanted to."
>
> "There, it is just as I said—you would not know any better; you have no idea of duty, command, obedience, they have no meaning for you. In your present estate you are in no possible way responsible for anything you do or say or think. It is impossible for you to do wrong, for you have no more notion of right and wrong than the other animals have. You and they can only do right; whatever you and they do is right and innocent. It is a divine estate, the loftiest and purest attainable in heaven and in earth. It is the angel-gift. The angels are wholly pure and sinless, for they do not know right from wrong, and all the acts of such are blameless. No one can do wrong without knowing how to distinguish *between* right and wrong."
>
> "Is it an advantage to know?"

"Most certainly not! That knowledge would remove all that is divine, all that is angelic, from the angels, and immeasurably degrade them."

"Are there any persons that know right from wrong?"

"Not in—well, not in heaven."

"What gives that knowledge?"

"The Moral Sense."

"What is that?"

"Well—no matter. Be thankful you lack it."

"Why?"

"Because it is a degradation, a disaster. Without it one *cannot* do wrong; with it, one can. Therefore it has but one office, only one—to teach how to do wrong. It can teach no other thing—no other thing whatever. It is the *creator* of wrong; wrong cannot exist until the Moral Sense brings it into being."

"How can one acquire the Moral Sense?"

"By eating of the fruit of the Tree, here. But why do you wish to know? Would you like to have the Moral Sense?"

She turned wistfully to Adam:

"Would you like to have it?"

He showed no particular interest, and only said:

"I am indifferent. I have not understood any of this talk, but if you like we will eat it, for I can't see that there is any objection to it."

Poor ignorant things, the command to refrain had meant nothing to them, they were but children, and could not understand untried things and verbal abstractions which stood for matters outside of their little world and their narrow experience. Eve reached for an apple!—oh, farewell, Eden, and your sinless joys, come poverty and pain, hunger and cold and heartbreak, bereavement, tears and shame, envy, strife, malice and dishonor, age, weariness, remorse; then desperation and the prayer for the release of death, indifferent that the gates of hell yawn before it!

She tasted—the fruit fell from her hand.

It was pitiful. She was like one who wakens slow and confusedly out of sleep. She gazed half-vacantly at me, then at Adam, holding her curtaining fleece of golden hair back with her hand....

Adam's eyes were fixed upon her in dreamy amazement, he could not understand what had happened, it being outside his world as yet, and her words having no meaning for one void of the Moral Sense. And now his wonder grew: for, unknown to Eve, her hundred years rose upon her, and faded the heaven of her eyes and the tints of her young flesh, and touched her hair with gray, and traced faint sprays of wrinkles about her mouth and eyes, and shrunk her form, and dulled the satin luster of her skin.

All this the fair boy saw: then loyally and bravely he took the apple and tasted it, saying nothing.

The change came upon him also.[8]

Distressing and shattering stuff, whatever its causes. Or its dubious justice.

The story moves on, takes us past the tree. And here another possibility emerges. Dishonesty may be a larger and more significant part of Adam's problem, and the Woman's. For no one seems to take responsibility in this story. When God asks Adam what he has done, the man implicitly blames both his companion, *and* his God: "*The Woman whom you gave* to be beside me . . ." he begins, deflecting the blame in a funny way, which may or may not miss the essential point.[9] With the Woman, it is nearly the same; she blames the serpent: "*The snake* enticed me, and so I ate."[10] She blames the serpent, but she would never think to blame the man. Mark Twain once again develops the point brilliantly, in "Eve's Diary." "He told on me, but I do not blame him," she smiles, "it is a peculiarity of his sex, I think, and he did not make his sex. Of course I would not have told on him, I would have perished first; but that is a peculiarity of my sex, too. And I do not take credit for it, for I did not make my sex."[11] Only the serpent says nothing, at least not in this version of the story; but then, God never asks anything of him.

Here is how Elie Wiesel, understands this curious and disturbing constellation of detail:

> [W]hy the punishment? The Midrash says they were punished not so much for having sinned as for having invented excuses and alibis.

---

8. This appears in the form of "Satan's Diary," which was appended to "The Autobiography of Eve" and written in 1901 or 1902. Published posthumously, these texts may now be found in Baetzhold and McCullough, *The Bible According to Mark Twain*, 65–67.

9. Gen 3:12.

10. Gen 3:13.

11. Twain, "Eve's Diary," in *The Bible According to Mark Twain*, 32.

> Adam placed the blame on Eve, and Eve placed it on the serpent.
> Their greatest sin was to have shunned their responsibilities.[12]

Merely to act out in disobedience is an act of the very purest immaturity, an act of early childhood; to accept responsibility, and moral consequences—and thus to create the *possibility* of beginning anew—this is the very promise and challenge of adulthood.

Gender makes responsibility even harder to gauge in this story—upon whom, after all, should we focus our moral attention? On Adam? Or the Woman? There is a tradition, which extends from Augustine to John Milton, one which insists that Adam, *un*like the Woman, was *not* deceived. He knew what he was doing, and why; he did it because he couldn't bear to be without Woman. He sinned in order to assure that they would stay together. The Romantics made a lot of hay out of that pretty modern idea. So did Twain, whose lyrical account of "Eve's Diary," penned shortly after the death of his own wife in 1905, concludes with one elegant, shattering line, Adam's very own, appended to her Diary: "Wheresoever she was, *there* was Eden."[13]

Wherever they were, punishment follows swiftly and certainly upon commission of a crime. It always does in the Book. But the connection between the crime and punishment is uncertain. The couple are mortal now; they will live as humans, apart from God, and then they will inevitably die. The man—the selfsame man, we recall, who was initially created to luxuriate in and to watch over this garden—now he will have to work in it, incessantly.

> Damned be the soil on your account,
> with painstaking-labor shall you eat from it, all the days
>   of your life.
> Thorn and sting-shrub let it spring up for you,
> when you (seek to) eat the plants of the field!
> By the sweat of your brow shall you eat bread,
> until you return to the soil,
> for from it you were taken.
> For you are dust, and to dust shall you return.[14]

---

12. Wiesel, *Messengers of God*, 27.
13. Twain, "Eve's Diary," in *The Bible According to Mark Twain*, 33.
14. Gen 3:17–19.

Adam's work is real work now, and will no longer have the pleasure it once presumably held for him. Is this why we garden, I wonder? . . . to recapture some small taste of what Paradise must have felt like, once upon a time? To recover something of the leisure and the exaggerated luxury that once went along, however mythically, with the tastes and textures of our food? Many students of the world's various conceptions of Paradise, especially Jungians and their ilk, believe this to be the case.[15] The garden as a memory of paradise lost.

The Woman is punished, too, of course; indeed, there has been a several-millennia-long tradition of blaming women for the temptations and corruptions of their men. The segregation of human societies along the lines of gender has wreaked much havoc on scripture and religion and culture. A brilliant novelistic account of this patriarchal-biblical world appeared a decade ago, and puts a fantastical new spin on such compelling ancient matters. Anita Diamant's *The Red Tent* describes an imagined world in which women who live together in such large patriarchal collectives naturally synchronize their menstrual cycles, and thus spend four days to a week together in seclusion, "in the red tent." It was here, Diamant invites us to imagine, that women kept women's stories and women's special wisdom alive, not to mention the medicinal and herbal techniques which often constitute their special expertise, in the all-important matters of birthing and of dying. The novel helps us to recall that women, at least until the modern period, had control of midwifery, of certain essential forms of healing, as well as the care for, and the laying out of, the dead.

Even Socrates bears a curious relationship to this ancient rule. While there is one tradition indicating that he was apprenticed to his father's craft of stonemasonry, this arch-philosopher identifies more with his mother's line, and his mother's line of work. She was a midwife (*maia*), he tells us, a big and burly woman whose name, Phainarete, points to the appearance (if not quite the reality) of virtue.[16] The art of midwifery is compared by Socrates to his own "maieutic art" of bringing *wisdom* to birth in others. In describing the art of midwifery, Socrates emphasizes the same techniques that Anita Diamant does: the drugs and incantations (*pharmaka kai epaidousai*); their powers to increase, as well as decrease,

---

15. Richard Heinberg's *Memories of Paradise* is an excellent source for much of this material.

16. Plato *Theaetetus* 149a–151d.

the pains of contraction and labor; their mastery of abortive remedies as well as procreative ones; and, curiously enough, their excellence in matchmaking too, since midwives know best which matches will be fruitful. Socrates compares his own rites, the verbal spells and soaring leaps of logic, to women's birthing arts. And still later, at the somber end of a life committed to such rigorous moral enquiry, Socrates usurps the role of women once again; he bathes his own body in preparation for its burial,[17] not wishing to leave this work to others.

It has been customary to view these details through the eyes of modern assumptions, ones presumably more informed by a feminist consciousness, however incomplete it is as yet. But it need not be so. For this same Socrates, who identifies with his mother and with the maternal arts of midwifery, also excluded his own wife from his final discussion with his friends,[18] fearing that a woman's inclination to tears would infect the men as well (later, they manage to find their tears well enough, all on their own). Socrates may not have been as hip as we want him to have been; he may be the first modern man who usurped women's prerogatives and prestige, not the first ancient man who celebrated them. It has been a commonplace for the modern western democracies to fault the Islamic world first and foremost on this point, for its alleged mistreatment and manipulation of women, their world of truncated religious and political possibilities. That there is *some* truth to the problem as posed is obvious. But the problem is hardly Islam's alone. There is, in fact, a long and ancient pedigree—a biblical as well as a classical pedigree—to the problem. And modern forms of women's "liberation" have hardly seemed as liberating as first promised or proposed. Christian fundamentalists in this country are as opposed to modern feminism's political and cultural goals as Muslim fundamentalists are in theirs.

And that, I think, is precisely what Anita Diamant worries about in the quizzical ancient world we see depicted in the book of Genesis. When the men took control of the writing and the religion, then women's stories either were rewritten, or else they gradually disappeared. None of this is to suggest that there was ever a conspiracy, or even a plan. Like most other empires, patriarchies simply happen; once they become self-conscious, then they are perpetuated, often by cruel design. It is for this very

---

17. Plato *Phaedo* 116a.
18. Ibid., 60a.

reason all the more important to listen to those they happened *to*. What is it like to be conquered, occupied, dominated? These are Diamant's poignantly Genetic questions. She elects to recover this elusive lost voice by zeroing in on the curiously peripheral character of Dinah, one of the silent daughters of Jacob. And so she begins:

> We have been lost to each other for so long.
>
> My name means nothing to you. My memory is dust.
>
> This is not your fault or mine. The chain connecting mother to daughter was broken and the word passed to the keeping of men, who had no way of knowing. That is why I became a footnote, my story a brief detour between the well-known history of my father, Jacob, and the celebrated chronicle of Joseph, my brother.[19]

The women are the herbalists in Diamant's story, the ones who tend their mother's gardens while the men wander with their flocks. It is a strange division of labor, since it makes women into the sole gardeners, matched well to women's punishment here, in Eden. The Woman is condemned to suffer enormously in childbirth, which is—from this biblical perspective, which makes names so decisively important—why we call the women's birth-travail a "labor." After the Fall, *everyone* labors.

And now something else rather strange happens. Adam's name we already know; it derives from the Hebrew word for "soil." But Eve had not yet been given a name; or rather, her name was simply "Woman." It is only now, *after* the Fall, that she receives a new name, the name we know her by, and it is Adam, not God, who gives it to her:

> The human called his wife's name: Havva/Life-Giver!
>
> For she became the mother of all the living.[20]

Her name is Havva, now. It is Eve in English, and in the Greek of the Septuagint, she becomes Zoe, the Greek word for Life. It is a surprisingly upbeat name, a startling way to conclude such an apparently awful story. Perhaps this couple really does understand the power of beginning again.[21]

---

19. Diamant, *The Red Tent*, 1.
20. Gen 3:20.
21. We should recall that Jacob, another prodigious name-giver, will disregard the dying wish of his own wife, who expired while giving birth to their last son. Jacob gives

The couple is expelled in sharp terms spelling the very gravest misfortune: "sent away from the garden of Eden, to work the soil from which they had been taken."[22] "Working the soil" has been a charter metaphor for this entire Creation account. But now, where does one go, after Paradise? Where else would a biblical couple ever go, save to the east?

> He drove the human out
> and caused to dwell, eastward of the garden of Eden [*miqqedem l'gan-'Eden*],
> the winged sphinxes and the flashing, ever-turning sword
> to watch over the way to the Tree of Life.[23]

I presume this, because we are not told specifically *where* this couple wandered. What we *are* told is what God did to prevent their coming back, back into the Garden. God places some rather terrifying equipment along the way the couple would presumably use if they ever tried to return. We are told specifically where God places that equipment—*on the east face* of the Garden of Eden. It stands to reason, then, that Adam and Eve wandered *east* when they were expelled from Eden in the first place.

This same pattern repeats itself in the next tortured human generation. Adam and Eve have two sons: Cain (Fox renders this as Kayin) and Abel (this name he renders as Hevel). Abel, we are told, became a shepherd, whereas Cain was a worker of the soil, a gardener. We are meeting that same, strange division of labor again: one gardens, or else one tends to the herds, but one cannot do both. Then the gardener murders the shepherd, his brother, for reasons that are far less clear than we would like them to be (Lord Byron wrote a fabulous play entitled "Cain" in 1821, a play in which he tried to resolve some of this mystery—Cain is a deeply Romantic and Mephisthophelean figure, in Byron's telling. A dear friend of mine, a scholar of medieval Judaism, still swears that Cain's the only biblical character he really wants to meet). There is jealousy, to be sure, the sibling-rivalry for the sparing attentions of a Father-God. But there is a strange gap in the text, just here, precisely where "Cain said to Abel

---

the child a different name than the one Rachel had chosen for him. She wanted him to be called Ben-oni, "son of my sorrow," but Jacob changed this to Ben-yamin, "son of the people," once his wife had died (Gen 35:16–20). Diamant faults Jacob for that, as she faults him for a great many things (*The Red Tent*, 208, 294, 311, 315).

22. Gen 3:23.
23. Gen 3:24.

his brother," something about going into a field.²⁴ Was he drawing his brother out into his own pasture? Or into Cain's own garden? Wherever the brothers go, instead of a meeting we witness a murder, the primal act of fratricide.

This is all very strange. Why, after all, should the gardener be the killer? Isn't it the herdsman who is normally the butcher, the one who works with blood? (Even the Greeks sacrificed grain far more than meat—blood sacrifice is always bloody, and unsettling). Everything seems upside-down in this story. And here again, the only clear thing, the remarkably swift thing, is the punishment God exacts after the crime. True to his lineage, Cain dissembles when God asks after his brother. He knows full well where his brother is, and he pretends not to know. In response to that, God curses him. There is no place, such as the Garden was, from which Cain can be exiled, but his trajectory still precisely matches that of his parents. He is driven away "from the face of the soil,"²⁵ exiled from his garden and exiled to the east:

> Kayin went out from the face of YHWH
> and settled in the land of Nod/Wandering, east of Eden
>   [qidmah-'Eden].²⁶

Just as Adam and Eve journeyed to the east into their own version of exile, so does their lost son, Cain. This much we learn, and one damning detail more. God curses Cain precisely as his father was cursed. Here is how Cain's legacy is to be remembered:

> And now,
> damned be you from the soil [min-ha'adamah],
> which opened up its mouth to receive your brother's blood from
>   your hand.
> When you wish to work the soil [et-ha'adamah]
> it will not henceforth give its strength to you;
> wavering and wandering must you be on earth [ba'aretza]!²⁷

---

24. Gen 4:8.
25. Gen 4:14.
26. Gen 4:16.
27. Gen 4:11–12.

Adam and Eve were exiled from Eden, to the east. Cain follows after them, tracing out this same, strange trajectory: *to the east.* So displaced, this family will never live upon or work the soil in quite the same way again. When next we pick up their story in any great detail, they will be a nomadic people, "wavering and wandering," like Cain. And they will be a transient people, much as Abel was. In fact, his name seems to mean something like "transcience," in Hebrew.[28] Philo, by contrast—who wrote in Greek, not Hebrew—insisted that Abel's name "means suffering all matters of mortality [*ta thnêta*], but taking delight in things immortal [*ta athanata*]."[29] According to Philo, it was a different name entirely—the name Hebrew (*Hebraios*) itself—which means "wanderer."[30] And the word he uses for wandering, *peratês*, has another peculiar connotation in Greek: it suggests wandering *away* from the east, *going to the west*. This, as we shall see, is the way Abraham went, not Adam.

The only good to come of this vast dislocation, Philo tells us, is that it creates the possibility of being a *kosmopolitês*, a more authentically cosmopolitan citizen of the world.[31] That is what Abraham's wandering, not Adam's, will make possible. But as every cosmopolitan wanderer worth his salt knows, the wandering itself changes things; it qualifies your attachment to home, your attachment to more local places. Sure, you can't ever really go home again, so they say. One day, you may cease even to desire it. I'm less convinced of the truth of that statement—it depends mostly on how deeply you've put down roots and whether you've gardened to do so. But one thing is certain in *this* story: in every way that matters, Adam's family has lost its roots, and ceased to garden—wandering aimlessly instead, in the east.

---

28. Everett Fox makes much of this fact in *The Five Books of Moses*, 25n2.
29. Philo *On The Migration of Abraham* [447] §74.
30. Ibid., [439] §20.
31. Ibid., [445] §59.

chapter five

WATER

The distant sail was now at hand, and once close enough, a man jumped down to swim and wade ashore. It could have been Dionysus himself, stepping from his raft, or Noah, released from his ark and relishing again the feel of sand between his toes. Noah and his vineyard seem remote from us now, and Dionysus, smiling languidly in the shade of a vine-sprouting mast—as he once had arrived in the Aegean, guided by dolphins—is a total stranger; yet both still influence our lives in ways we scarcely recognize and rarely understand.[1]

...

You can read the soil in much the way that you read a book. Five years ago—and here again, it just so happened to take place in the fall—I undertook a major landscaping change on the periphery of my own ever-changing garden plot. I installed a series of wooden steps that joined the upper grounds on the west slope to the lower garden next door, to the east. I terraced in the entire slope, shoring up some of the rougher terrain with wooden walls, trucking in several loads of dirt from several local neighborhood construction sites, and slowly, slowly, the new borders took shape. I hedged it all in with flowerbeds, planting them abundantly in a luxurious exaggeration of springtime bulbs, gorgeous autumn flowers,

---

1. Asher, *Vineyard Tales*, 277.

and a few of those rarer ones that grace the place with blossoms all summer long. There are pheasant-eye narcissus, a sort of daffodil-with-make-up-on, which I imported from a dear friend's home in New Hampshire (he was once a professor, then a friend, to whom I dedicated the first book I ever wrote, and I mark his passing two years ago with a grief I do not yet know how to give voice, nor how to give to the ground)—these took awhile to adapt to the deadening southern heat. There are generous plantings of salvia, whose name calls "salvation" to mind, and speaks to it in the outrageous drama of its nearly continual blooming. Much of the border is defined now by fire-tipped irises; a few simple bulbs planted in the fresh soil trucked in to receive them now produce literally hundreds of new shoots each year—amazingly, I've been forced to cut them back, and to parcel out the bulbs as gifts, four times in as many years). Snapdragons bear a name which stymies the poet in me, though I suppose when the light is just right, in late afternoon and early evening, their nodding heads of red, white and yellow do look vaguely like the heads of miniature dragons—without the fire. Dianthus is a Greek name meaning "double-flower," a fitting name for anyone who has ever seen this loveliest and most delicate of all my garden flowers. In hybrid form, it provides unique splashes of color available in no other way. And finally, there are the pansies, an almost inevitable presence in every North American garden, their smiling, nodding faces never failing to make us pause and ponder. That's what their name comes from in fact, an Anglicizing of the French term, *pensée*. Shakespeare had another name for them; he called them "Love-in-idleness." Love and leisure. . . . I like to think on all of that, the nomenclature and the histories they hide, as I wander here.

Toward the conclusion of these casual projects and new plantings, I elected to sink a pretty white archway in the new soil to either side of the central stairway, and I planted wisteria, which finally, throughout the later summer months, began to climb up and over the latticed enclosure. I took pains to weave the new vines through the intricate latticework, and so it grew. In the space of four years, they have matured into elaborate vines, gorgeously purple when in bloom and fabulously fragrant. Their flowering has come to serve as an important symbolic marker of early springtime to me, now.

Many friends warned me off of the wisteria, and at least one of them, an extraordinary writer herself, who was then in the process of coordinating a special volume of the *South Atlantic Quarterly* devoted to "Gardens and Landscapes" (in which I first began to think about such bookish matters),[2] made an intriguing biblical connection—likening this plant to sinning humanity in the first Garden. Wisteria is a dangerous weed in southern climes, I know. It sends out new vines everywhere, chokes out neighboring plants, and generally smothers as it goes. Once you've planted it, and once it's established itself, it's nearly impossible to be rid of it. So wisteria may seem a lot like Adam and Eve, and even more like Cain and his long-suffering brothers: once they were planted in the Garden, then cast out into its easterly surroundings, they threatened to take over. So God uprooted them, cast them out and away. To the east.

I've never had much trouble with my wisteria, to be honest, though I do still see the point. In my neighborhood, it's hard not to see it, for the wisteria is everywhere, climbing fifty feet and higher up into some trees. It chokes out whole groves of trees in the few remaining vacant lots, just as surely as Japanese Kudzu does on any open stretch of southern interstate. And it proves just as threatening, to any serious gardener . . . or so they say.

Sure, the wisteria grows like mad, and sure, it sends its shivering tentacles into pretty copses of flowers I am working hard to nurture and preserve. Mine has even managed to stretch itself, incredibly, across a wide space of open air and into a nearby crepe myrtle tree. But the point is, you've just got to stay on top of it. With regular pruning, the wisteria does just fine. In fact, wisteria is one of those rare plants which, the more you cut it back, the more it rewards you, devoting still more of its energy to luxurious blooming in the springtime. The aroma, for that short span of two delirious weeks in early April, is worth any amount of tending and trouble. Its perfume literally fills my home. God presumably understood this. In any event, God is portrayed as an aggressive and prodigious pruner, in the beginning.

I had originally wanted to plant a grape arbor here, not wisteria, but grapes came late to my garden, just as they come later in the Book. Roughly a year after that major landscaping effort I just described, I met a fascinating Lebanese doctor who worked in a local hospital, and who'd come to hear a lecture on the modern Olympics that I happened to be giving in town. We chatted after my talk, and he invited me to his home for coffee. The following weekend, we sat and talked for hours in his backyard under

---

2. See Crozier, "After the Garden?"

a gorgeous canopy of grape leaves, an arbor that provided his surest and most eloquent link to a homeland. He had brought the cuttings with him from Lebanon, and they'd obviously prospered here—both the planter and his vines. I took five cuttings from them myself, and am amazed still at how they've taken hold. I've given gifts of cuttings, now, to three other households, and I'm forced to prune back the grapevines twice a summer, and once again in the fall. They've proven to be far more work than the wisteria, which is telling. Pay close attention to a garden, and you may find that the real work lies fairly far from where you'd anticipated it.

They are also a strange variety of grape, one engineered to produce leaves, but no fruit. They flower into pretty green leaves of incredible delicacy, and have the ideal softness and texture for making those delicious stuffed grape leaves whose rich flavors always remind me of the Mediterranean. And yet, as I say, these vines produce no fruit at all. It's too bad Noah didn't know about them, in a way, although the whole course of Mediterranean history would be different, had he known.

Moving off to the north slope, where the terracing trails off into thicker growth, I installed some stone steps, constructed from pieces of that wonderful north Georgia granite that is so characteristic, so pretty, and so widely available here. Some last occasional flowers planted alongside these steps pretty well marked the end of this large landscaping project that, needless to say, occupied me off and on throughout the fall and well into the ensuing winter.

One thing I had not considered, as I so thoroughly altered the contours of the local landscape, was water-management. It was the Romans who understood the importance of this, with an intensity and investment of energy that the Greeks could never match. Hydraulic engineering operates on a single, elegant principle: keep the good water inside, and the bad water out. This Noah knew.

When at last the heavy rains came in January and February—moisture piped up from the Gulf of Mexico on the wind, then dumped precisely here by the bucketfull—water collected in a standing pool at the base of my new stairwell. A stair-*well* it had become, in very truth. It seemed a well worthy of the biblical patriarchs. And eventually—as it gradually became clear that I would not fix this, I suppose—the water found its own way out, carving several small channels that, while dry and wadi-like now, will once again turn to rivulets and full-blown streams in a short span of months.[3] After the fall, like it or not, comes the win-

---

3. I found one last thing particularly interesting about that water slowly collecting

ter. And water, I have learned, cannot be fought, only managed with greater or lesser skill, and accepted with a certain kind of patience, "like a river unafraid of becoming the sea."[4] The ancient Chinese classic, *Tao Teh Ching*, is a marvelous compendium of such water-wisdom. So is the Confucian *Book of Changes*. The Romantic poets spoke often to this idea. And some of it is echoed in the Book as well. Here's yet another lesson that Noah, the last great cultivator we will meet in these strange genetic tales, learned to his great hurt.

The story of the first six chapters of the Hebrew epic we know as Genesis is a story of decadence, pure and simple, of steady and almost inexorable moral decline. Human beings, as Job will put it later, are "born to trouble as the sparks fly upward." We are "mortal, born of woman—few of days and full of trouble."[5] And so humanity proved to be, in the beginning. In six relatively short, shattering chapters we witness human disobedience to the very first divine command, human expulsion from its Paradise-Garden, the first murder (a fratricide, no less), followed by a veritable *explosion* of violence upon the earth. There is so much violence, in fact, that God seems to repent of ever having created at all. First, of course, there is the problem with all these people:

> Now YHWH saw
> that great was humankind's evildoing on earth
> and every form of their heart's planning was only evil all the day.
> Then YHWH was sorry
> that he had made humankind on earth,
> and it pained his heart.[6]

at the foot of my new stairwell in the wintertime: for reasons I cannot begin to fathom, when finally the water found its own way out, it flowed, dewy and direct, *to the east*.

4. I take this lovely image from a gravestone in the pretty Acattolica Cemetery in Rome. It is inscribed on the grave of "Gregory Corso, Poeta," who died on the 12th of January, 2001.

Not far from him lies Shelley, whose grave boasts similarly that "Nothing of him that doth fade/ But doth suffer a *sea*-change/ into something rich and strange."

And finally there is Keats (whose grave I've already mentioned), buried in the adjacent garden, whose tomb reads, simply and at his own embittered request, "Here lies one whose name was writ in water."

5. Job 14:1.

6. Gen 6:5–6.

But there also seems to be a problem with the very soil itself. There is a long-standing tradition, evident in many cultures' originary myths, that the evil-doing of humankind effects not only human society, but nature and the land as well.

> Now the earth had gone to ruin before God, the earth was filled
>   with wrongdoing.
> God saw the earth, and here: it had gone to ruin,
> for all flesh had ruined its way upon the earth.[7]

So God floods this badly damaged earth—with rain and more rain, forty days and forty never-ending nights of the stuff. As one of the Dead Sea Scroll documents, *A Commentary on Genesis*, describes it: "On that day all the fountains of the great deep broke open and the windows of the heavens were opened."[8] This description of the Flood reminds us of the first biblical account of Creation, the Mesopotamian one, the one with all the water. It seems almost as if God is *reversing* the act of Creation here, a *de*creation which opens up the very floodgates and sluice-works that God had taken such trouble to construct. God tears down the levees, turns on the spigots, opens all the windows in heaven . . . *and it rains*. The Creation itself seems undone, or very nearly so. Our connection with Eden, with the Garden, and with the bloodline of Adam and Eve is nearly severed, in any case. From now on, as the rabbis were quick to notice, the human family is conceived as a tribe of Noachites, not Adamites. The severity of what has just been done, while muted in this account, is inescapable to any subsequent audience that feels as it reads, especially in North America after the carnage unleashed by Hurricane Katrina in 2005.

But God spares Noah and his family, as we know. Pruning, cruel as it often seems, is always done with an eye to *saving* something else.

> God said to Noah:
> An end of all flesh has come before me,
> for the earth is filled with wrongdoing through them;
> here, I am about to bring ruin upon them, along with the earth.
> Make yourself an Ark . . .[9]

---

7. Gen 6:11–12.
8. This passage may be found in Wise, Abegg Jr., and Cook, *Dead Sea Scrolls*, 275.
9. Gen 6:13–14.

Noah spares, at God's command, seven pairs of every ritually pure animal, and one pair of every impure animal. (How human beings knew the difference, at a time well *before* ritual cleanliness had been explained to them, is one of the many puzzles the rabbis attempt to sort through so creatively in that marvelously Jewish tradition of Question-and-Answer we know as Midrash, Commentary, and Talmud). When finally they achieve their landfall, and "the face of the soil was firm" again,[10] Noah sacrifices some of these ritually clean animals to God, and the odor of the feast-to-be pleases the divine sense.

So God makes a covenant, a *b'rith*—one of the most significant of all divine gestures in this religious tradition—with Noah, *and* with Noah's descendants, *and* with every living thing. God promises never again to destroy the earth—*with water*. God obliges everything to respect life in all its forms, but most emphatically in the blood, where life's force is thought especially to reside. Blood *does* seem to have an almost eerie magic power about it, after all . . . one thinks of one's own blood, bright and warm and wine-red, bagged by the Red Cross or Crescent . . . and one thinks, tragically, of scenes where people stand in need of such blood, accidents, bombings and shootings, the whole wretched theater of elaborate human cruelty that first prompted me to these biblical musings some years ago. God provides a physical sign, the rainbow, to commemorate this signal event that re-establishes a connection between mortals and their God. "My bow I set in the clouds," God says, "so that it may serve as a sign of the covenant between me and the earth."[11]

Literally, God "cuts" a covenant, in Hebrew. It's strange how often the ritual and commemorative sign for a covenant involves a *cutting* in the Book. I recall the shock I felt in a museum dedicated to the olive and the history of its cultivation (it all started in what is now a non-wine zone, ironically enough, the long borderland between Turkey and Iran). The museum is in a little Umbrian village called Torgiano; in it, you see just how many different forms and types of cutting implements human beings have developed simply to prune back their grapes and olive trees. Why, when the sign of a covenant is *not* a cutter, must it become a weapon? Here it is a bow, a weapon set in the sky, after the rain. And soon, it will be a pruning-knife, set to its own strange work of cutting.

10. Gen 8:13.
11. Gen 9:13.

Human beings do next what human beings perhaps do best. They start over; they begin again. In the face of such a global devastation, there seems little else *to* do. Gardens have a special way of teaching that lesson to us. Gardens have a way of teaching many lessons, if we have the ears to hear them and the eyes to look.[12] One of my favorite illustrations of this simple gardener's truth comes from the Louisiana novelist, Walker Percy, in a rambling poetic remembrance of his uncle, William Alexander Percy, himself the author of an Old Southern classic, *Lanterns on the Levee*. Here is what the novelist remembers of his uncle, the memoirist:

> I remember him in his garden—a famous one—hands in pockets, frowning down on something, perhaps an iris with root rot. He took solace in his garden and from it drew human lessons. Once, as he put aluminum sulphate on his azaleas, because azaleas, of course, need acid soil, it came to him in a flash: some people, too, require acid soil! Of course! This explained a friend of ours, Miss A, who for reasons that escaped everybody thrived on tragedy and controversy. Thereafter, Miss A was no mystery. Uncle Will gave her controversy cheerfully, acid soil aplenty, and the two of them got along famously ever after.[13]

Each season brings its own unfolding dramas of dawning and destruction: from diseases and belligerent pests, to various animals that seem intent on rolling over new seedlings—whether in seriousness or at play, crushing them all the same—to hail and thunder and flood. I do not think that I have ever planted a single time in all my years of gardening, in *any* season. Gardens simply don't work that way. One is forced to begin anew, ever and again.

Noah looks for all the world like a second Adam, and through him, the earth is peopled, and cultivated, again. Just as there were two accounts of the initial Creation, so there is a doubled human origin. Our common ancestors are both Adam and Noah. And now, the sacrifice complete, the covenant "cut," Noah plants himself a garden.

---

12. One especially sensitive student of the garden was Henry Mitchell, whose weekly musings in the *Washington Post* were later collected as *The Essential Earthman*, and are chock full of such glorious little lessons.

13. Percy, *Signposts in a Strange Land*, 66.

> Now Noah was the first man of the soil [*'ish ha'adamah*]; he planted a vineyard.
> When he drank from the wine, he became drunk and exposed himself in the middle of his tent.[14]

Hebrew stories move in stops and starts. This story is noteworthy for how suddenly it starts, then shifts on a dime. It is about to get stranger still. Noah is lying, presumably dead-drunk and naked, in his tent. The Septuagint puts this all in the passive voice, as if it all had simply happened to him and no one were responsible: "and he became drunk" . . . "and he became naked."

Noah's youngest son, Ham, apparently saw his father in this embarrassing state. And he told his two older brothers, Shem and Japheth, what he had seen. By way of weird response, they carry in a coverlet over their shoulders, walking backwards, so as not to gaze upon their father's nakedness at all. We are meant to remember that Noah is a second Adam here, I think, and so we are meant to remember that Adam's troubles had something to do with nakedness and inappropriate covering as well. (The linkage between these stories is brilliantly exposed on Michelangelo's Sistine Chapel ceiling panels: from Creation, to Adam, to Noah's drunkenness, *nudity* is the key).

That said, this story goes straight from the strange to fully bizarre. When Noah wakes up in the morning, he realizes what his youngest son has *done* (*'asah*) to him. The Septuagint says the same thing. Yet no mention had been made of Ham's *doing* anything; he had only *seen* his father, that was all. Noah's response to this unexplained thing he knows is equally odd, equally sudden, and equally unexplained: "He said, 'Damned be Canaan / servant of servants may he be to his brothers!'"[15] Noah does not curse Ham directly, but rather curses Ham's *son*, a young boy by the name of Canaan. And he curses him for something entirely unstated, something that the boy's father had presumably *done* to his grandfather.

This is the sort of story that gave the source-critics and rabbis a scriptural field for endless tilling in the soft soil of Torah, the first five books of the Hebrew Bible.[16] It looks for all the world like some sort of

---

14. Gen 9:20–21.

15. Gen 9:25.

16. This specific material is helpfully summarized by Graves and Patai in *Hebrew Myths*, 120–24.

"independently circulating oral tradition," a story that in this case has been almost deliberately garbled. What did Ham (or Canaan) *do* to his father (or grandfather)? Parallels with neighboring myths and legends suggest themselves at once: there is no shortage of castration-tales in the annals of prehistory. One thinks of Cronus and his brothers, castrating their father, Uranus. And one thinks of Zeus, with his brothers, castrating Cronus, in turn. Was this bizarre Noah-story intended to be another one—the story of usurping brothers who conspire to castrate an unwitting father? An unanswerable question, of course—and it is surely significant that Philo, so full of questions and answers about Genesis (he has a long book with that title, as I have already indicated, one that was originally written in Greek, but that survives primarily in an especially rare Armenian copy), never dares so much as to pose this one: What did they *do* to Noah? Philo takes great pains to worry about where Noah found a grapevine after the Flood;[17] he goes to even greater lengths to explain that, while Noah drank wine, he did not drink it to excess.[18] He worries a great deal about nudity and its symbolic meaning.[19] But he asks not one word about what Ham *did*.

As interesting as source-critical analyses of the biblical texts sometimes are, they often operate on the assumption that the biblical authors woodenly copied over their sources, or else that they stapled various stories together in the crudest fashion. They fail to see the ways in which these men and women were gardeners as well as scribes, how well-versed they would have been in the loamy metaphors of planting, grafting, and cross-pollination. The biblical authors were highly skilled, highly reflective persons who were in the business of re-telling old tales to make contemporary meaning. Their work is seldom simply sloppy (though it sometimes is).

So what can we say about this strange and garbled gardener's tale, the story of the first *'ish ha'adamah*, or "man of the soil?" Well, for starters, it is the very *last* thing we are told about Noah. He lives on for three hundred and fifty years after the Flood,[20] but we do not hear one word more about him. He has served his narrative function, whatever it was,

---

17. Philo *Questions and Answers on Genesis* 2.67.
18. Ibid., 2.67, 68, 73.
19. Ibid., 2.69–70.
20. Gen 9:28.

and the story moves on without him. But how does it move, and where is it going? The Book moves on to the manifold of human generations, and the re-peopling of the planet. It attempts to explain which of Noah's descendants went where, and why the peoples today are named as they are named. It focuses on the eponymous founders of the various human tribes living in the so-called "Fertile Crescent." And that seems to be what the biblical author here is interested in: not an embarrassing castration-story, but rather the cursing of *Canaan*. This was presumably of great contemporary interest to his or her audience; it would serve to justify, among other things perhaps, the perfectly horrible biblical treatment of the Canaanites that is soon to come. These bizarre ethnic tales can thus be made to seem exceedingly contemporary, and highly destructive. There are roots of Modern racism in such tales, and of genocidal imaginings. Old Southerners, in fact, were to justify their own forms of race-based slavery by identifying black Africans precisely as descendants of Ham.[21] But they had rabbinic warrant, alas, for some of these strange claims.

It all seems deeply disturbing, immoral, and ugly to us today. It can make the Book seem ugly, too, although it is not difficult to see in such racism the great failure to embrace the metaphors of grafting that are also so central within it. Perhaps we see what we want to see. This seems all-too-contemporary, in a world where *Blut* is still too often linked to *Boden*—blood drawn to soil, as it was with Cain—despite the previous century's devastating experiences with the crazy logic of fascism, and a world where identity—religious, national, and other—has become a source of such apparently endless contestation. Our ancestors are, as often as not, a source of conflict rather than inspiration to us. And that makes our connection to a "tradition" something of a problem, too. Worrying about all of this has been a large part of what the Modern, western democracies have been trying to do well for several centuries. They are trying to re-think, not to un-think, their traditions.[22] What democracy's enemies worry about is that this effort makes any reasonable commitment to tradition, especially to a *religious* tradition, seem unreasonable or impossible. The world is warring over these worries even as I write.

---

21. This story is brilliantly told by my good friend, Thomas V. Peterson, in *Ham and Japheth: The Mythic World of Whites in the Antebellum South*.

22. In navigating through these debates, I have been much informed by Jeffrey Stout's latest book, *Democracy and Tradition*.

But I am, as the Book sometimes does, getting ahead of myself. For time moves rather oddly in a garden. Past and present can seem almost primordially linked. There is a general flow, a quiet cadence, a fluidity: things planted long ago bloom each spring, seeming new every time; the annuals die, and need to be replaced; and there is pruning, always there is the pruning. That is the rhythm of a garden, the invitation to inhabit time in a different way, more in the way that artists and monastics do. How might an artist—for certainly a gardener ought to be an artist—reconfigure these ancient debates about ancestors, identities, and time? There seems no more relevant biblical worry than this, given the political and polemical worries of our day.

chapter six

GRAFTING

We are like the mixers of the wine. And there are two springs beside us, to the left and to the right. One stream has honey, the honey of pleasure. The other has water, the water of wisdom, sober and pure and healthy. We have to learn to mix them, as well as we can.[1]

...

The sun has given way, first to the clouds, and now to a light drizzle as I take my mid-morning break, a second cup of coffee still in hand, out and over the dampening ground. I am paying particular attention to three new rows of garlic that I transplanted last year. I want to be sure that they remain well watered while they establish themselves. God has seen to that, I note, as a largish raindrop lands in my cup with a palpable #plop.# These pretty, moist rows of garlic never fail to make me smile. They represent—ironically, and far more so than the Lebanese stranger's grape vines—my strongest link to a former lifetime and a figuratively different world.

For six years in total, I spent my summer months on the northwest tip of Crete, working on the Greek-American excavation of what has since proven to be an enormous pirate harbor called Phalasarna. Long days of digging concluded somewhere between two o'clock and three o'clock in

---

1. Plato *Philebus* 61c.

the afternoon, when we all reassembled at the excavation-house—twenty-five men and women living together in four small rooms—for a meal, a great deal of wine, to be followed by that delicious Mediterranean late-afternoon sleep. One of the workers had brought an impressive bundle of small, fresh young garlics with him from his own garden, tilled in the courtyard of his home in the lovely Venetian harbor of Xania, still my favorite harbor-town in all of Greece, as Crete remains my best-loved Greek island. Gerald Asher's lovely little collection of *Vineyard Tales* does a wonderful job of establishing the centrality of this richly blessed and singularly beautiful island in the ancient *and* medieval arts of viticulture and oenology. Someday, I would like to dedicate a book to the mystery of my affection for this island.

The wine was known as Malmsey, and seems to be making a quiet modern comeback. Ancient mythology imagines Crete as a vast ancient clearing-house where wine made its way from Asia to the west. Excavations of several Bronze Age Cretan sites—called "Minoan" after the legendary Cretan King, Minos—speak to this impressive ancient art. When the Venetians established themselves and gained an economic foothold on the Greek mainland in the thirteenth century, first at the gorgeously austere coastal fortification called Monemvasia, the fort served as a major port of transit for Cretan wines that then made their way back to Italy—via another pretty fortress, near to where I was, on Corfu—and beyond. The name of this first Venetian fortress later gave its name to the wine: Malvasia in Italian, Malvoisie in French, Malmsey in English. And the market for Cretan wine really exploded between 1330 and 1669, when the last Venetian outpost on Crete fell to an Ottoman siege that had lasted for nearly two decades. It was that two-hundred year Turkish occupation which wreaked such havoc on the vintner's art in Crete, an art that is only now being resuscitated. Winebibbing, we will recall, became an issue of the greatest importance in the last chapter with poor old Noah; it will prove to be again.

Each of our meals at the excavation-house began in much the same way: glasses filled, we toasted one another's health, reviewed the day's small successes and comic interludes, and then, as the others brought salads and sauces of various sorts to the table, and as I refilled the glasses, my friend tore several garlics from the bundle which hung over the central lintel-stone, and laid them at the center of the table for all of us. I gradually learned to acquire a taste for this delightful midday drinking, as well as what was, to him, an ancient and much-loved culinary habit. My newfound Greek friends, some of them anyway, literally punctuated bites of fresh fish, octopus and calamari, not to mention the local tomatoes and greens, by popping entire garlic cloves into their mouths. One bite, one clove, one broad Mediterranean smile. These are surprisingly smallish garlics, their tight little cloves fairly bursting with a distinctive flavor to accompany the bite. Before the first season of digging was over, I occasionally nibbled on cloves all by themselves, on site. At season's end, in what proved to be my last year at Phalasarna, I asked my friend to bring me several garlics from his garden, to take home with me to mine. He did. And so did I.

My first task upon returning here, to Atlanta, was to break up those magical herbs, and thus to make a row of them in my own garden. They seem to flower—for reasons, and with a rhythm, I cannot explain—two and three times in the year here, and they have expanded impressively, bumping up now against neighboring beds I traditionally devote to melons and greens. So it was that, unwilling or unable to consider pruning them back, I dug out the majority of them, used some for cooking (although they have a noticeably different flavor, I discovered to my considered surprise, in this foreign, exile ground), and broke the rest apart for re-planting. Three small garlics became, in the short space of three years, three large and impressive rows, all waiting to be harvested or replanted in the soil. Oddly, I never nibble on them with my meals here; that only works in the high heat of summer, and only seems to make sense in Crete. Diet, too, is an emphatically *local* thing.

Noah had three sons, I am recalling, as the rain begins to fall somewhat harder now. And through them, the world itself was peopled again. Shaking dewy drops from my hair, I retreat indoors to my desk, to think about this some more.

After those outrageous biblical rains comes the story of the peopling of the planet again. To tell that story, the Bible moves, much as one would expect by now, to the east. Here, in the tenth chapter of the book of Genesis, comes one of those impressive, and dizzying, genealogies for which the Book is well known. Noah's eldest son, Shem, was blessed by his father at the same time that the grandson, Canaan, was cursed. Then there follows one of those long genealogical lists that *seems* to operate according to the strictest rules of primogeniture. We trace lineages through the lines of eldest sons, and that is all. No younger sons are mentioned by name, and no daughters are mentioned at all. That's just the way such "patriarchal" societies seem to work. It is not precisely the way God works, however, as we shall see—and that becomes a matter of some importance, too.

So, Noah had an eldest son named Shem, and Shem—tired perhaps of all the monosyllables—named his eldest son Arpakhshad, a real biblical mouthful. Arpakhshad had a son named Shelah, who had a son named Eber, who had a son named Yoktan. And here, for whatever reason, the Book pauses momentarily—perhaps to allow us to catch our breath, perhaps for reasons more mysterious than this. Yoktan had thirteen children, *all* of whom are mentioned by name . . . and this family catalogue is not the only thing we are told.

> Now their settlements went from Mesha, then as you come toward Sefar, to the mountain-country of the east [*har haqedem*].[2]

Punctuated by this now-to-be-expected reference to "the east," this really is the end of the story, of one extended and impossibly complex genealogical story (though it is not the end of the line). We can tell this, because the story is concluded, not once, but twice—with another sort of textual seam. These long and very precious genealogical lists, of which literate priests in every generation presumably have been the proud custodians, are concluded once again: "These are the Sons of Shem," we are told, in rhythmic, sing-song Hebrew:

> after their clans, after their tongues,
> by their lands, after their nations . . .[3]

And, lest we forget from whence Shem has come, we are handed still one more genealogical tidbit: "These are the clan-groupings of the Sons of Noah, after their begettings, by their nations."[4]

It is intriguing to notice this sudden biblical attention to the matter of clans (*mishpechôtam*, in Greek it is *phylais*), and to languages (*leshônô*-

---

2. Gen 10:30.
3. Gen 10:31.
4. Gen 10:31.

tam, in Greek it is *glôssas*) and to lands (*'artzotam*, in Greek it is *chôrais*). But I'm struck especially by the weird and unformed notion of "nations," given how very contemporary a problem this conception is. I have no idea what "nations" meant in that distant age: *gôyêhem* is the Hebrew term for it here, and it's translated into the Septuagint's Greek pretty consistently as *ethnê*, from which our word "ethnic" derives. It's a distinctive human grouping of some sort.

This much we can say with confidence: this has quite suddenly become a story about ethnic diversity, the story of a distinctly human kind of dispersion, the vast descendancy of Noah slowly and prodigiously repeopling the planet. They do so, as we have seen, by moving east again. And it is to the east that we continue, on our wide-wandering biblical way.

> Now all the earth was of one language and one set-of-words.
> And it was when they migrated to the east [*miqqedem*] that they
> found a valley in the land of Shinar and settled there.[5]

You probably already know what comes next; it follows fairly logically upon the story of human dispersion and ethnic diversity.

Next comes the story of the Tower of Babel—which means Babble, in Hebrew, and which ancient Christian commentators like Orosius and St. Jerome located in the legendary city of Babylon—built just here, in the ancient land of Shinar and the modern nation of Iraq. The result of this failed attempt to storm heaven is, precisely, even further human dispersion and even greater ethnic diversity. People now are not only more broadly scattered across the land; their languages are no longer mutually intelligible. There are increasingly borders built between us. And translation itself has emerged, finally, as a poignant and urgent human problem. The reader of the Book cannot fail to notice this. Nor can the gardener who grafts as well as plants.

But this story raises another interesting problem for the Book's storyteller. It is suddenly no longer possible to tell the story of everyone—what language, after all, would there be to tell it in? The Book has created a problem for itself—or rather, it has found itself confronted with a peculiar human problem. It resolves this problem by zeroing in on one man, a mysterious man named Abram. We will not try to tell the story

---

5. Gen 11:1–2.

of the entire planet and all its peoples anymore; we will endeavor to tell a story *about* the planet, a story *representative* of all its human inhabitants and their Creator, by telling one story, the story of a single man and his singular family. That is the way things always seem to work in Genesis—by paying careful attention to locale, and by proclaiming God's interest in *local*, rather than global, spaces. God really does act like a gardener in Genesis, especially when God is grafting.

Who is this man, Abram? The Book, not surprisingly, gives us his genealogy first. It is a genealogy we have met before, up to a point. We will remember that Noah had a son named, monosyllabically, Shem. And we may remember that Shem preferred trisyllables, naming his son Arpakhshad. And Arpakhshad had a son named Shelah, and Shelah had a son named Eber—and it is he, oddly enough, who may be the eponymous founder of this curious tribe of the "Hebrews."

Now, the last time we walked through these complex family trees, we talked about Yoktan at this point, whose descendants migrated "to the east." But Yoktan, it turns out, was not the eldest son of Shelah; another boy by the name of Peleg was. The names, for whatever reason, are *all* disyllables now: Peleg to Re'u, Re'u to Serug, Serug to Nahor, Nahor to Terah, and Terah—lo and behold—had three sons, the eldest of whom *appears* to have been Abram.

Terah's three sons are named Abram, Nahor, and Haran. It has always seemed a pretty detail to me that Terah named one son after his own father, Nahor—they still do this on Crete, but it is always the *eldest* boy who gets the grandfather's name. Was Nahor, then, possibly the eldest son, coming *before* Abram, who was next? God often looks to *second* sons in Genesis, and this is what some late midrashic commentators on this passage conclude: that Abram was the divinely favored *second* son, not the first born at all.

Terah's sorrow comes quickly; he lives to experience what every parent most dreads. Terah witnesses the death of his own child, Haran, who died unexpectedly, while the family was still living in a city the Hebrew text consistently calls *'Ur Kasdim*, or "Ur of the Chaldeans."[6] That's presumably because there were many cities going by that name, just as there are many cities hereabouts named "Greenfield" and "Greenwood" . . . and "Peachtree." This Chaldean connection is especially interesting. We saw

---

6. Gen 11:31.

special use made of Chaldean chronologies by our friend, Bishop Ussher, when he was calculating the historical age of the world. The Chaldeans were especially renowned for their astronomic knowledge, something that many accounts claim Abram inherited, and passed on. He understood the sky as well as the soil, on this view—understood where his God was, as well as wherever he himself was working.

Whether to get away from his sadness, or simply to be on the road again, Terah decides to leave the city of Ur. He takes his son, Abram, with him, as well as Abram's young wife, Sarai.[7] There is a remarkable hymn dedicated to Sarai's beauty which may be found among the *Genesis Apocryphon*, a curious body of texts found among the Dead Sea Scrolls in 1947. Sarai's beauty is a matter of the gravest importance to the Book. Here is how one of the Egyptian Pharaoh's advisors, Hyrcanus by name, describes his first vision of her, when the couple first arrived in Egypt:

> How beautiful is Sarai;
> Her long, fine, glossy hair,
> Her shining eyes, her charming nose,
> The radiance of her face!
> How full her breasts, how white her skin,
> Her arms how goodly, how delicate her hands—
> Her soft palms and long slender fingers—
> How lissom her legs, how plump her thighs!
> Of all virgins and brides
> That beneath the canopy walk
> None can compare with Sarai:
> The fairest women underneath the sky,
> Excellent in her beauty;
> Yet with all this she is sage and prudent,
> And gracefully moves her hands.[8]

The transplant family with the beautiful young bride also takes responsibility for the orphaned son of Haran, a younger nephew to Abram by the name of Lot. And together they set their eyes on *ha'eretz Kana'an*, the fabled land of Canaan.

---

7. Who is also his half-sister at Gen 20:12.
8. As quoted by Graves and Patai in *Hebrew Myths*, 144.

But they never make it. They end up settling instead—or else merely stopping, the story is unclear—in a city called Harran (actually, the name of the town is identical to the name of Terah's lost son, in Hebrew—we just add a second R to it, to distinguish the two). And it is here that Abram's father, Terah, died—still on the way, as it were. But the journey of this nomadic family, we soon learn, is just beginning. In fact, the very next thing that happens is that God—YHWH, the only God who ever was or will be, in the Book—comes to visit Abram personally. And the very first thing God tells Abram is that it's time to be moving, again. "Go-you-forth," YHWH commands:

> from your land,
>
> from your kindred,
>
> from your father's house,
>
> to the land that I will let you see.[9]

It is terribly provocative that God does not tell Abram precisely *where* to go; God simply orders him into exile. Or rather, God commands Abram to be a wanderer again. And Abram, we will notice, elects to continue on the path his father had begun. He presses on to the land of Canaan.

It is an uncanny detail: Almost without our being aware of it, this entire Genesis-narrative, so global in its scope and so dizzying in its details, has just undone itself. For fully twelve chapters, we have been moving carefully and continually eastward, but now, all of a sudden, the Book has managed a narrative double-take. The arc of the story has been arrested, and reversed. In order for Abram to get to the land of Canaan, he needs to turn around, and to move decisively *west*. The entire biblical trajectory has doubled back on itself, decisively reversing course, with implications for subsequent biblical developments that will be profound.

Christianity bears a far more strained and complicated relationship to this idea than Judaism does. It does so, in part, because of its storied and complicated relationship to Islam. Christianity, under the aegis of Paul's Gentile gospel, moved from Jerusalem even further to the west. The most casual survey of the names of the cities to which Paul wrote his most memorable letters—Ephesus, Thessaloniki, Corinth and Rome, among others—tells the tale. This new religious force, which always met with, at best, a lukewarm acceptance in its Judean place of origin, really

---

9. Gen 12:1.

took off in transplant soil, then grafted itself to local traditions, in the west. Greece and Asia Minor were the most fertile gardens for the spreading of this new religion; still later, Europe became its slaughterhouse.

One of the most dramatic about-faces ever managed by the world of Christendom was that redoubtable masque of Frankish and Venetian empire-building we call "the Crusades." The very first of them, which set off overland from Europe in 1095, and culminated in the capture of Jerusalem and an orgy of bloodletting four years later, makes this all very plain. Here is how the chaplain to Baldwin the First, Bishop Foucher of Chartres, framed his case:

> We, who were people of the West, have become citizens of Tyre and Antioch; we have already forgotten the place of our birth, and many do not know it at all. Some of us have houses and servants in this country, which we will give to our descendants as their heritage. Others have married women who are not their countrywomen, but are the natives of Syria, Armenia, or are even Saracens, who have received the grace of baptism. Some tend to their vineyards, others to their fields; they still speak in different tongues, but they already begin to understand each other; those who were poor in their country, God made rich; those who did not even have a manor, now rule over cities. Why should they return to the West, if they do so well in the East?[10]

We can discern the arc of troubled movement here, the strange twists and turns that come of narrative doubling, then doubling back again. Christians attack Muslims and Jews. Muslims then attack their Christian occupiers. So the westerners eventually leave the east and return home. This all has a vaguely Greek feel to it. The Trojans kidnaped Helen. The Greeks destroyed Troy. The Persians later invaded Greece, unsuccessfully, twice, but did great damage on the way. Alexander the Great returned the favor, invaded Persia, and won it, for a while. As Greece's last Nobel Laureate, Odysseas Elytis, sees it, "every era has its Trojan War."[11]

God gardened east. God's fallen pests and human co-workers were exiled still further to the east. Cain continued to the east; so did Noah and his descendants. It was *Abram* who doubled back and headed west, obey-

---

10. As quoted in Herbert, *Barbarian in the Garden*, 132.
11. Elytis, *Maria Nephele: A Poem in Two Voices*, "The Trojan War."

ing God's mysterious command. Christianity amplified and intensified this westward trend. Its peoples even crossed an ocean, in time. But first the faith doubled back on itself once again, returning with a vengeance to the east. Wielding a sword. And a cross. And fire.

chapter seven

FIRE

> It seems to me in times like these that our soul is like a book. . . . Memory mixed with perceptions, and the feelings they inspire, seem to me virtually to write words upon our souls. . . . And there is another artist in our souls at such times as well . . . he is a painter, one who paints images of the words which were written there, on our very souls.[1]

. . .

Fire feels like fall, and smells like it, too: burning piles of fallen leaves, freshly raked from well-groomed suburban lawns; roiling bonfires before Friday night football games, lighting up shining high school faces all across the state; the first soft kindling in the fireplace, a warm anticipation of the more serious winter months ahead, carbonized wood and charcoal frozen into place by the heat. For all these reasons, and more, fire feels like the fall—but not necessarily to the gardener. Gardens point to paradoxes we otherwise miss: the mixture of hot with cold, the pruning and preservation, the vast mixture of it all.

Paradoxes being what they are, fire evokes late springtime, and even the high heat of summer, to *this* gardener. And fire is indelibly linked to pruning. At least twice each season—once in the mid-to-late spring, and once in the very heart of summer, normally right around our July

---

1. Plato *Philebus* 38e–39b.

4th national holiday—I conduct a big burn. By then, there is plenty of fuel to burn—as the characteristic wildfires in the western United States each year attest. I normally try to stockpile all of the branches that have been pruned from all of the trees on the property, and leave them piled high under a tree somewhere, so that they can dry out and be ready for this big, summer burn. The grape vines, as I have said, require severe cutting back two and even three times a year now, in their maturity, and those pretty tangles of dark wood and long leaf turn gradually brown and brittle on top of the pile. There are other, more random pieces of fuel that inevitably accumulate in a garden: branches blown down in the high winds of the first summer thunderstorms; tall shoots of vegetables and vines from the first spring planting, gone to flower and then to seed by early summer, requiring still more pruning back—all in order to clear a space to start over in.

The neighbors' reactions to these big, controlled burns are radically different in the summer and in the fall. In the fall, they require no explanation—they look and smell just right, seeming a fitting accompaniment to the cooler seasons. We all tend to associate such fires with the fall. But in the summer, they seem frankly bizarre. I must confess to a real liking for them, myself. And they serve multiple purposes, in a garden. I have the very fondest memories of last July's burning—especially this morning, now that it's come suddenly cooler and greyer here. Blazing midday summer heat, compounded by waves of smoke and furnace-blasts of warm wind—I am reducing an enormous pile of pruning to sweet ash, ready for summer tillage. By carefully choosing the spot for a summer burn, you can accomplish a great deal. The ashes—and it is during this summer burn that I choose to clean out my fireplace, adding those sacred winter leavings to the mix—make a marvelous supplement to organic, composted soil. The eggplant seem especially to like it; so do the melons. Burning off all the flotsam and accumulated debris from a well-wooded plot like this one also contributes a sense of order to the place that it rarely has in this season, an order I know cannot last. It's virtually a spring-to-summer-cleaning for the out-of-doors, and just as thick with ritual. Finally, given the hardy persistence of stringy crabgrasses that always threaten to take over this garden, a controlled burn is the easiest way, and really the only way I know, to keep them under control. Once their roots have been established this surely, burning is the only way left to prune them back. I repeat this important parable often enough to myself: there are many plants which are a lot harder to control than wisteria, and for them, there is nothing for it but the fire.

When it's all done—fires extinguished, smoking ashes worked in to the blackened topsoil, sweet, woody odors clinging to the entire area, corners cleared and properly edged—*then* the garden is ready for its second big planting of the season. As I say, you need to cut, and even to kill, to create a space to start over in.

After Abram's father, Terah, died in Harran, the quiet trio of Abram, Sarai, and Lot pressed on to the west. It must have been a strange trip, and the Book describes it strangely. No sooner do the three arrive in Canaan than YHWH makes one of those startling visitations that mark Abram's wanderings just as surely as Abram's wanderings mark the land. God promises the land (how much of it is never specified, and there are no maps—so it's just whatever he can see) to Abram's descendants as a perpetual inheritance. Abram builds an altar, a site for sacrifice, for this mysterious promissory God at a place called Shechem. And then Abram continues to wander south, into the Negev, looking for greener pastures, until famine finally pushes the family further south to its brief, bizarre sojourn in Egypt, where Sarai's beauty gets everyone into a thicket of new trouble.

It is when the three return from Egypt that our story commences, again. Ever since God's first visitation, Abram has had the touch of Midas. His flocks and his people have swollen to numbers the land cannot support, since Lot has prospered as well, blessed by his simple proximity to this silent man-with-God. The rival tribes of herdsmen take to quarreling, and Abram—a man of quiet discernment, surety in action, and few words—proposes to Lot that they part now, while it can still be managed amicably. He offers Lot the choice of where he wishes to settle. We will not be surprised to learn what Lot chose.

> So Lot chose for himself all the plain of Jordan.
> Lot journeyed eastward [*miqqedem*], and they parted, each man
>   from the other.[2]

Lot went east. And there is no surprise in the Book's making a point of telling us that. But there is special interest in seeing *why* Lot chose the way

2. Gen 13:11.

he did. Lot, as it turns out, chose the well-watered plain near the Jordan River. The valley's vast fertility doubtless reminded him of the land in the Garden of God (*k'gan-YHWH k'eretz*); it also reminded him of those fertile Egyptian fields that narrowly hug the Nile.³ We have already seen the strong suggestion in this Book that human beings are not cut out for Paradise, that *struggle*, everything we now associate with "labor," is an essential part of the human story. If that is in fact the case, then Lot's choice is disastrous. He is not only trying to get back to the east, he is reminiscing about a Garden from which we have been permanently exiled. He is trapped in the very worst and most paralyzing kind of nostalgia. As we will soon see, it is a disastrous choice.

But before we see why, the Book returns quickly to Abram. The camera seems always to have this man in view, even when he is not on-screen. No sooner has Lot gone off to seek his *eastern* fortune, than YHWH comes to visit Abram again.

> YHWH said to Avram, after Lot had parted from him:
> Pray lift up your eyes and see from the place where you are,
> to the north [*tzaphnah*], to the Negev [*vanegbah*], to the east
>   [*vaqêdmah*], to the Sea [*vayammah*]:
> indeed, all the land that you see, I give it to you
>   and to your seed, for the ages [*ad-ôlam*].⁴

This seems a pretty strange promise. We have just seen Lot wander off into what he believes will be his *own* eastern inheritance. Now we are told that Lot will not inherit any of it—east, west, north or south.⁵ Abram will, "for the ages." So Abram is instructed to walk the length and breadth of this inheritance, just to get the feel of the land and its promise.

> Up, walk about through the land in its length and in its breadth,
>   for I give it to you.
> Avram moved-his-tent and came and settled by the oaks of
>   Mamre, which are by Hevron.
> There he built a slaughter-site to YHWH.⁶

---

3. Gen 13:10.

4. Gen 13:14–15.

5. I especially like the rhythm of this line in the Greek Septuagint: *pros borran kai liba kai anatolas kai thalassan . . .*

6. Gen 13:17–18.

Obedient as Cadmus, and just as widely traveled, Abram does as he is told. The amount of ground that Abram covers in his long sojourn on this earth is truly astonishing, when once we consult the map. His journey began in Ur of the Chaldeans. He has been to Canaan, and to Egypt, and back again. It must have been something of a relief for this man, after his long travails, to settle, after a fashion, by those shaded oak trees at Mamre. Silent though he normally is, we can see subtle signs that Abram grew attached to this place, even cast a careful eye on the idea of owning it, eventually.

But Abram is unable to sit in his inheritance for long. Lot, as we saw, chose his plot poorly. He tried to regain a Paradise that is gone for good. He just so happened to settle in the vicinity of two cities called Sodom and Gomorrah. (Sedom and Amora is how Everett Fox renders their Hebrew names for us). Philo insists that the first name, Sodom, meant either "blindness" or "sterility," a fanciful etymology if ever there were one.[7] Lot eventually settles in the first of these fortress-cities, whether cursed by blindness or sterility or both. But first, he faces a more immediate problem. War breaks out between several local fiefdoms. An alliance of four city-kingdoms (that of Shinar, Ellasar, Elam, and Goyim) faces off against an alliance of five others (Sodom, Gomorrah, Admah, Zeboyim, and Bela—that last city was also known by the name of Zoar). Caught in the middle of these warring factions, Lot and his people are taken captive, along with all the other spoils of Sodom and Gomorrah. When Abram hears of it, he marches off in full battle array to rescue his nephew. And he does. In fact, Abram drives the forces he has scattered well to the north, beyond Damascus. Only then does he return with Lot and the loot—loot which was stolen from the king of Sodom, who expresses his gratitude in exaggerated terms of obeisance.[8] Abram, having none of it, returns to his home, glad, we cannot help feeling, to be done with the whole sordid business, and that whole territory. That territory, we will remember, that he left to Lot. And we probably all know what happened next: God destroyed the place—with fire.[9]

Of all the many notorious and wrenching stories in the book of Genesis, this is in some ways the most notorious. (It had such an endur-

---

7. Philo *Questions and Answers on Genesis* 4.23.
8. Gen 14:1–24.
9. Gen 19:1–26.

ing impact that later biblical authors returned to its imagery, and even filled in the matter of the rape, at Judges 19:1–30). All this to say that "Sodom and Gomorrah" name one of the best-known stories in the Book, and for this very reason, we probably do not really understand it very well . . . because we think we already know what the story is about. When we know something so well that we feel no need to study it, we tend to miss what we should most clearly be digging to find. This is the first wisdom a garden implants: steady patience, clear-eyed confrontations with what needs doing, relentless and careful attention.

The Christian tradition later invented a sin, and called it "Sodomy."[10] Until four years ago, the Georgia State Legislature accepted the invention, in their notorious "Sodomy statute" (No. 16-6-2), whose constitutionality was actually upheld by the US Supreme Court.[11] This forced left-leaning members of the Georgia State Legislature to rewrite the law, which they neglected to do for a decade, but have done now. "Sodomite," in short, is a derogatory term, not the name for a citizen of the city of Sodom, but rather for a (presumably male) homosexual or pederast.[12] So it was that the city of Sodom eventually became associated in the Jewish mind with same-sex-sexuality, later gave its name to a medieval Christian sin, and finally established it as a crime deemed worthy of punishment with fire.

To be sure, the sexual resonance in this story is pronounced, and bizarre in every way. But we should pay careful attention to specifically *how* it is bizarre, and *why*. Two messengers of God visit the city we know is doomed; only Lot offers them hospitality. When the men of the town, young and old alike, learn of it, they stampede Lot's house, batter the door, and demand "to know" (*yada'*) the visitors, a clear biblical euphemism for a carnal kind of sexual knowledge. (This is true in Greek as well, where *syngenômetha* invokes a kind of "knowing with" that is not-so-subtly sexual). Lot—and this detail ought to be especially startling to a modern audience—offers the townsmen his two virgin daughters in place

---

10. Whose strictly medieval history is charted out by Mark D. Jordan in *Invention of Sodomy in Christian Theology*.

11. In *Bowers v. Hardwick*, 478 US 186 (1986). The High Court changed its mind, and its tone, in the summer of 2003, in a far-reaching decision called *Lawrence v. Texas* [539 US 558 (2003), argued in March and decided in late June], which invalidated such sodomy laws in Texas, and by clear implication, in the other eight states that still possessed them.

12. Oddly enough, this is how Philo already understood the meaning of the word in *Questions and Answers on Genesis* 4.37–38.

of the visitors, since he can apparently abide the violation of the rules of hospitality far less than he can accept the violation of his own children. It is strange that this story should ever have been read as a moral story, since it clearly suggests that to rape a daughter who has been proffered is permitted, whereas to rape a male visitor in one's home is a crime. And for this crime—actually, for the intent alone, since the men of Sodom are not permitted to do anything—the city and its surroundings are turned to a smoking ruin.

An elaborate prophetic and midrashic mythology later attached itself to the name of Sodom. Its inhabitants were alleged to be obscenely rich, horribly ungenerous, theatrically cruel to visitors, and utterly pansexual. They were, in a word, *pagan*—for this is how Jews and Christians and Muslims have all too often summarily dismissed a "pagan" world they seldom felt the need to know or understand. The *sexual* excesses of pagans were especially underlined by later Jewish and Christian polemics.[13] That should already make us suspicious of the theatrical display of sexual appetite in *this* story.

An earlier tradition suggests that what troubled God so deeply at Sodom was not homosexuality *per se*, nor perhaps even the possibility of rape, but rather what clearly troubled Lot himself: the egregious and shocking face of *inhospitality*. This surely mattered far more to most ancient peoples than "sex" did; we moderns are the ones who fixate so obsessively on sexual matters—the false face of Freudianism, perhaps. It is significant in this regard that vaguely canonical Jewish texts like Ecclesiasticus 16:8 and Book of Wisdom 19:13–14 castigate the citizens of Sodom for excessive pride ("He did not spare the neighbors of Lot / whom He loathed on account of their arrogance," says the first) and their utter disregard for the rules of hospitality ("they justly suffered for their wicked acts / for they practiced a more bitter hatred of strangers," says the second). The prophet Ezekiel condemns Sodom for her lavish living and inattention to the poor:

> This was the guilt of your sister Sodom: she and her daughters had pride, excess of food, and prosperous ease, but did not aid the poor and needy. They were haughty, and did abominable things before me.[14]

13. For more on this strategy, see Knust, *Abandoned to Lust*.
14. Ezek 16:46–49.

Prophets like Isaiah and Jeremiah, Amos and Zephanaiah, all use the name of Sodom as synonymous with a general and pervasive spirit of wickedness.[15] Even Jesus seems to associate both cities with the violation of well-accepted norms of hospitality, and the vastness of their destruction, not with some specifically sexual excess.[16] By contrast, the Qur'an seems to associate Sodom with precisely such sexual sins,[17] but it remains uncertain how serious a violation this was thought to be. Sometimes, such Sodom-sins are framed as an abomination in the Qur'an, while at others they are simply the result of ignorance, something requiring instruction and divine guidance, but certainly not fire.

In short, we are cast back upon a somewhat surprising possibility: that this story, which clearly does have a pronounced, and deeply disturbing, sexual component, is nonetheless not a story about same-sex sexuality, nor really about "sodomy" in the modern sense at all. As I have said before, it may well be our own modern obsession with sex and sexual identity that invites us to read these ancient stories in these modern ways.[18]

The story, in any case, ends as oddly as it began. Lot actually seems *un*willing to leave this doomed city even after he has been warned; God's angels literally have to push him out the door, or rather, outside the city gates. Lot lacks the unflagging obedience of Noah, and of his uncle. He loses his sons-in-law, who do not heed his warnings and remain behind, and he loses his wife when she gazes back behind her, sees the city in flames, and is turned to a pillar of salt. None of this is explained to us, and none of it makes much narrative sense. Lot had prayed for one small town named Zoar (or Sêgôr, in Greek) to be spared (this was one of the five cities that had originally been in an alliance with Sodom and Gomorrah), so that he might re-settle there. But now, after what he has just seen, Lot is clearly afraid to live in any town, and so he retires with his daughters to a nearby hillside cave. That cave was later commemorated by a hillside Byzantine church, and has recently been excavated in the

---

15. See Isaiah 3:9 and 13:19, Jeremiah 23:14 and 49:18 and 50:40, Amos 4:11 and Zephanaiah 2:9.

16. Matt 10:14–15, and Luke 10:10–12.

17. Qur'an 7:81, 26:160–70, 27:55.

18. One of the earliest and most influential presentations of these conceptual difficulties was John Boswell's *Christianity, Social Tolerance and Homosexuality*, esp. 91–117, and 335–53, a book I still teach and admire.

plateaus of southwestern Jordan. (The site, De'ir 'Ain 'Abata, is a sixth-century monastery recently excavated and published by Dino Politis of the British Museum).

It is here in this cave that, in a strange inversion that echoes the last story we heard about Noah, Lot's two unmarried daughters make him drunk with wine, so as to become pregnant by him.[19] One drunk father had presumably been castrated by one of his sons (or else by all three). A second drunken father is now raped by his two daughters. And their incestuous issue are named Moab and Ben-Ammi (or Amman, in Greek), eponymous founders of the two southern tribes—the Moabites and Ammonites—which gave the fledgling Israelite kingdom such unrelenting trouble in a later age. "Ammonite" became almost synonymous with the very worst of enemies, in King David's day. But it was no more specific a term than Sodomite.

Now, it would be a gross misrepresentation of these stories to suggest that they are not about sexuality, at least in part, or that they do not wish to paint a clearer picture of what kinds of sexual practices are permissible and which are not. Incest is not—though it happens and though different cultures define appropriate kinship relations in very different ways. Rape is not, at least among men—though it happens a great deal. Male homosexuality seems not to be either—though this seems to have been a fairly standard practice among the more overtly bisexual non-Hebraic peoples surrounding Abram and his kin. There is a very clear prohibition of same-sex sexuality, among the men at least, in some later Jewish texts.[20]

But the issues addressed by these ancient stories are not modern, and their worries are not exactly ours, either. So here: the story *begins* with a harrowing episode of attempted rape. It moves on to a father's apparent willingness to submit his own daughters to such rape, then concludes with them raping their drunk and unwitting father, in turn. Yet the larger narrative cycle concludes, unexpectedly, with politics—with the justification of Israelite territorial policies and expansion in a much later, imperial period—at the time when some reflective Judeans were presumably trying to come to terms with what *their* emperors, especially David and Solomon, had unwittingly created. As we see still today, sadly, such terri-

19. Gen 19:30–38.
20. Saul Olyan's "And With a Male You Shall Not Lie the Lying Down of a Woman," provides a wonderfully lucid analysis of these passages.

torial conflicts are far more volatile, and far more violent, than our more mundane and often self-indulgently bourgeois arguments about sex tend to be. Those twinned towers in New York were not assaulted because of the allegedly lax sexual mores of North Americans. It had everything to do with war and with politics, with occupied territories and with land. It had something to do with the vast Arabian Peninsula, home then to large US military bases, and something else to do with the long-suffering land of Canaan.

chapter eight

LAND

Look at Abraham: was he not a resident alien [*paroikos*] in another place? And Jacob: was he not enslaved, first in Syria, then later in the land of the Palestinians, then in his old age in Egypt? Doesn't Moses say that he led them out of the house of enslavement in Egypt "with arm stretched forth"? And after their sojourn in Palestine, did they not change their fortune more than a chameleon changes its colors, as the saying goes—now ruled by judges, now enslaved to other tribes? And when they finally got a king ... but I leave that aside. For God did not wish them to have kings, as the Book says, but he was compelled to it finally, and warned them that they would be badly ruled with kings. Still, they lived on the land and gardened in it for a little more than three hundred years. Then they were enslaved again—first by Assyrians, then by the Medes, still later by the Persians, and finally now by us. Even this Jesus whom you preach and proclaim was a subject of the Caesars.[1]

. . .

There finally comes a break in the drizzle, and it gives me the opportunity, coffee finished now, to head back outside to tidy up a few things in the garden. The birds, as I think I mentioned, have been continually after

---

1. Julian the Apostate *Against the Galileans* 209e–210a.

the grass clippings, and several rows of younger shoots—brussel sprouts and broccoli, mustard and collard greens, Swiss chard and kale, cabbages and pretty assorted young lettuces—are now almost entirely hidden from the diminished autumn sunlight. The gaping holes in the mossy surface, looking for all the world like wartime potholes from the previous century's terrifying new ways of waging war, have revealed some weeds beginning to take root under the canopy of clippings, and it seems to me that the soil between the rows could do with a turning. I've also noticed one other area, near the garden's corner, where I have allowed the more stubborn and persistent crabgrasses to spill over into a vegetable-patch. Not a problem, really; it just looks sloppy. I will want to cut that back, too—with a hoe and a handpick today, not fire.

Happy at the thought of several small, manageable tasks ahead of me this afternoon, I walk next door into my neighbor's backyard, struggle, as I do each time, to remember the combination of the lock on her basement door (successfully so on a second try), and enter the deliciously dry interior. Most of my gardening tools—well, *her* gardening tools—are here. As is the all-important lawn mower. Both the water heater and furnace are located in this basement as well, so the area is always delightfully dry and warm no matter what the temperature outside may be. Today, despite the crisp first chill in the autumn air, is no different. I linger in the dry heat, deliberately selecting the tools I will need for the tasks of this day, then wander slowly back outside again.

It may seem strange to have the run of a neighbor's home this way. And surely it is, by most modern North American standards of local living, with its fairly ferocious commitment to privacy and interior spaces. I used to live in this house, years ago. The house, which was playfully named "Kamp Karma" shortly before I moved in, is an interesting modernist structure, boasting two adjacent living quarters joined by a long, latticed runway. I rented the cottage from its owner when I first returned from my two-year sojourn in Greece. This house, then, was the very first home of my homecoming, and I have always felt a special attachment to it for that reason, among other more obvious ones, which this book is attempting to describe. I began keeping a garden semi-seriously here, too. Each year it has expanded, chewing up ever-greater portions of the owner's yard. She has taken all of this in gracious stride; we have agreed, without ever really saying so, that I will take care of her yard, cutting the grass, planting flowers, and the like—things I enjoy doing anyway—in recompense for using her land, virtually as I see fit. These sorts of agreements have a casualness about them that is hard to define—hard even to understand, from the outside. There are no contracts signed, nor lawyers consulted—and, still more important, there are no clear borders. Cultivating land can erase borders just as surely as it can draw them.

After three years spent living next door, my present home became vacant. I had long laid a covetous eye on it. When the couple, who were friends of mine, prepared to leave, having bought a home of their own outside of the city, I leapt at the chance to replace them. My new apartment is considerably larger, boasts both a fireplace and an enclosed greenhouse, ideal for growing spices and other aromatic green things indoors in the winter. This move also offered the intriguing possibility of moving onto a larger piece of property—new ground ripe for cultivating—and had the added attraction of contiguity with the ground I had already been working for some years. It was the right move at the right time. So I moved. And within the space of six, short-long years, the entire local environment has been slowly transformed by my presence in it. Then it was that I dared to imagine larger projects: the wooden and stone stairwells, attendant new flowerbeds, trellises, wisteria and grape arbors, other things. I have already talked about most of them, but have not found the right words to describe the quiet pleasure of watching them come, slowly and amazingly, into being each spring.

There is another interesting dimension to all of this, one which especially concerns me here, and that is the absence of borders to which I've already alluded. I have run each and every one of these projects by my former landlord and my present one. Happily, they are good friends, both to me and to one another—and that is important. No one seems to know exactly where the border that divides the one property from the other lies. No one seems to care very much. This seems profound and significant, somehow: I literally no longer know where the line lies, the one that separates my old home from my new home, my new garden from my former one, her property from hers. And it is precisely a *garden* that has blurred those lines, once and for all.

Now, I do not want to make this all sound homier than in fact it is. I have to confess to an occasional, though recurrent, fantasy: one in which I win the lottery and buy *both* pieces of property, with all their attendant structures, making them more definitively, or at least more legally, my own. The uncommon generosity and quiet courtesy of this well-fortuned and happy southern neighborhood has not done away with simple human covetousness—least of all, my own. Still, there is something else here that seems to hold all of that in check. And that mysterious something seems to have a lot to do with the land, with the special attention and feeling of connection to local space, which has played such a large part in the stories I am endeavoring to re-tell. None of us really owns any of this. We are—in our finest moments, and beyond the mad cacophony of cupidity—custodians of the place, nothing more. Some notion of mortality, I'd guess, serves to keep our natural acquisitiveness in check, too. Mortality gave human beings their first morals well before God gave them a Law—that's what the Book implies. So the Garden was also humanity's first school and law-court. Where we were condemned. *And* set free.

Cutting the grass back from that southeast corner of the garden where it was overgrown proved to be a more complicated undertaking than first I had believed it would be. More than a simple pastime, this has turned into a real project. The soil is soft, damp, especially well turned and aerated here, so that the grass has rooted itself pretty firmly in an astonishingly short time. I feel as if I've only just finished weeding here, yet here I am, at it again. It takes the better part of an hour to clear the line of the enclosure, to get all of the stray roots and rhizomes cleared away. I have to work slowly and deliberately, because this corner of the garden is not only a flowerbed. It is also a cemetery.

We seldom hear of Abram's animals, other than the general observations of how many he had, how productive, and very occasionally, how pretty they were. We are never told—what must surely have been the case—that Abram had his favorites (God, after all, *plays* favorites in this strange Book), and that the death of certain well-loved animals brought him nearer to grief. Thus far, I have contented myself with a description of this garden, this house, and this yard . . . but a house*hold* also includes its animals. And my neighbor's household, like my own, has been richly blessed with the modern suburban version of an ancient flock.

Here, in this special corner of the garden—the very first one I cut and cultivated, as it so happens, which is strictly devoted to the cultivation of flowers, now—are buried three originary members of this household as well as some later stragglers and add-ons. It is an important testimonial, a reminder of the august passage of time. I have lived here long enough by now to watch two generations of pets come, and then go just as poetically. Pets are impossible to describe in any simple way, of course, and their owners seldom are able to speak of them at all. There is too much to say; each one warrants a chapter of its own. Like the biblical authors, I am struggling against the fateful *in*ability to be everywhere at once, to tell the story of all by . . . well, by telling everyone's story. The storyteller must find some other way to proceed. So God focused on Abram. And I focus on the three original members of the tribe next-door.

"Shadow" was big and brawny and slow-moving, and black as midnight from nose to tail. Proud possessor of a mellow poet's soul, gracious to a fault, Shadow was a dog willing to let the cats have the run of the place, willing to let them steal the household show, forever playing Abram to their Lots. Shadow, however, was quick to protect them, and us, if ever a stranger came too close to the home. Again, very much like Abram, he would thoughtlessly march into battle in defense of those he believed had been left in his care. He barked ferociously at any new visitor, although he never was able to sustain his feigned anger or venomous anxiety for long, and he never, ever bit anyone, to my knowledge. His bark really was the worst of it—a harsh ululating curdle, especially fervent whenever a police or ambulance siren came wailing nearby—and it morphed into happy, tail-wagging greeting soon enough. He was a saint among dogs, who waged a long, lingering battle with cancer without ever so much as a whimper of complaint, even after he was unable to walk, or finally, even to move. He lies under a large copse of white and red geraniums now, turning his death into a beauty as rare and exquisite as his life had been.

"Epiphany," as her name suggests, was regal, aloof, every bit a princess, quiet and alluring. I should have called her a white cat, although I see now in a slightly faded photograph that she was thoroughly speckled with pretty splotches of black and tawny brown. She was quiet, something of a loner, only rarely consenting to be petted. But when once she did climb into your lap, she would purr and luxuriate as only the truly aristocratic soul can, simply and serenely abandoning herself to pleasure. I think of her almost as a sort of Isaac, caught beneath her larger companion's—well, beneath his *shadow*—but as interesting, and occasionally even more interesting, in her own right. She survived Shadow by a matter of months only, dying as effortlessly and as elegantly as she had lived, then joining him in marriage to this same soil.

I must confess that I never bonded to a second cat, named "Farnan," as I had to the others, never really got the feeling for him. Farnan had a transient air about him; he came to live permanently on the land shortly after the others had died, and I feel certain that those ghosts and expectations were impossible for him to overcome. Farnan is hard to describe, especially at this long mental remove: a mingle-mangle of different colors, with no single home to call his own, nor even a single owner—the animal equivalent, perhaps, of a pagan failing to admit a single God. I suppose that makes him a lot like Lot, as I've never been able to discern any particularly strong sense of Lot's character in the Book, either. Farnan, in any case, survived his forebears by one single year, and now lies gathered among them, almost indistinguishable, in that same sacred stretch of soil, punctuated by bursts of autumn color, where I am lingering at the weeding now.

The rest of Abram's story—after this decisive parting with Lot—may, for our geographical purposes, be fairly easily told. Content as he is in the generous promises YHWH has made to him, he is still without an heir. So desperate is he with the implications of Sarai's continued sterility, that she herself invites him to have a child with her maidservant, an Egyptian woman named Hagar. Abram does so, and they conceive a son whom he names Ishmael, eponymous founder of the tribe of Arabs, according to one later midrashic tradition. But only one. It's dangerously misleading to try to derive too much modern identity from these ancient stories. That is a leap of logic that tends more often than not to lead to bloodshed.

God reappears in more solemn guise next time—calling Himself *El-Shaddai*, which means something like "God, the Almighty"—and this *all*-mighty God reiterates, for the third time now, promises about the land and its inheritance that have all been made before. This time, however, certain important details are added.[2] First and perhaps foremost, Abram's and Sarai's names are changed, through the addition of another consonant, which is to say (as I said earlier today), by adding one more syllable. Abram becomes Abraham, and Sarai becomes Sarah.[3] Abram also receives a physical sign—the curious ritual marker of male circumcision (*m-l*, Gen 17:10–14)—which is mandated to be a perpetual mark of this still highly familial covenant (*b'rith*). That very same day, at the overripe age of ninety-nine, Abraham circumcises himself and all of

2. Gen 17:1–27.
3. Gen 17:5.

the people in his extended household. It is hard to conceive, harder still to imagine it.

Then Abraham sets to wandering again, returning to the Negev Desert, well to the south. I can't help but wonder what he made of the smoking ruins he saw in the land Lot had coveted. True to God's promises, Sarah spectacularly conceives in her ninetieth year, bearing a son whom the couple is instructed to name Isaac, a name that suggests "he laughs." He is Abraham's second son, of course; and he, not the first child, is the apparent child of promise. That is just the way God tends to things among the biblical patriarchs. It's often how one tends a garden, too—second plantings can be especially fraught with significance. You grieve your losses, then you move on. But there's precious little to laugh about where Isaac is concerned. His story is inseparable from the Akedah,[4] that awful and paralyzing sacred tale in which the very child whom this God has given is now threatened with a sacrificial death. More horribly still, by our more modern lights, Abraham seems prepared to sacrifice the child, just as he has been ordered to do. He is as dutiful as Cadmus, and at times, very nearly as blind. Spared at the very last moment, Abraham and the child—who must by now be wondering about the wisdom of his father, and the justice of his father's God, not to mention this awe-full covenant—return to their people. And at this point in the story, a detail not without its special poignancy, the special piece of loveliness who was Sarah dies.[5] What, after all, is there left for her to do or say, now that her own child has proven to be replaceable?

Still, there seems no getting away from it: with this one grotesque exception, and maybe even because of it, Abraham elicits a unique fascination in the Book. He is so endlessly fascinating as a character that two other world religions—both Christianity and Islam—have tried to claim some sort of family relation to him, if only a relation by adoption, in the Christian case. Arabs claim a connection to Abraham through his first son, Ishmael, just as Jews do through his grandson, Jacob. Christians later came to believe that anyone—even the Greeks—can be adopted into God's strangely familial way of doing things now, through the work of yet another one of Abraham's prolific descendants, Jesus, son of Joseph.[6]

---

4. Gen 22:1–19.
5. Gen 23:2.
6. Matt 1:1–16.

And it fell to a nineteenth century adoptee, a Christian from Denmark of all places, to puzzle most profoundly over the desert-like quality of the Akedah.

As Søren Kierkegaard (1813–1855) describes the matter, with rare philosophical eloquence and the finer sensibilities of a poet, even in the Akedah, Abraham is weirdly compelling. I'd *know* him in an instant, Kierkegaard tells us in his 1847 classic, *Fear and Trembling*, though I'll never *understand* him. Kierkegaard emphasizes this repeatedly, almost as if he's trying to find just the right way, just the right word, with which to say it. Failing that, he just *keeps* saying it, over and over again—sort of like God promising God-ly promises to the man. "Abraham I cannot understand;" Kierkegaard puzzles, "in a certain sense I can learn nothing from him except to be amazed."[7] So the Akedah is fundamentally about amazement. Maybe. Or perhaps, Kierkegaard adds, it is about the utter strangeness (along with the amazement) of *faith*: "he who walks the narrow road of faith has no one to advise him—no one understands him."[8] Or maybe the right response isn't exactly amazement, so much as one of *admiration*: "I cannot understand Abraham—I can only admire him."[9] What Abraham's lifelong career is decidedly *not* about, for Kierkegaard, is philosophy or theology, much less what we traditionally think of as ethics. To make good on that argument, he returns to his old arch-rival and straw-man, the Berlin philosopher, Georg W. F. Hegel (1770–1831). Or rather, he turns to those self-satisfied Danish Hegelians, who also claimed to be Christians, and who claimed with such smug facility to have "understood" both Hegel's "System" of philosophy, *and* Abraham's willingness to murder his own child. These claims share a common failure—the failure of humility and real understanding.

> It is supposed to be difficult to understand Hegel, but to understand Abraham is no small matter. To go beyond Hegel is a miraculous achievement, but to go beyond Abraham is easiest of all. I for my part have applied considerable time to understanding Hegelian philosophy and believe that I have understood it fairly well; I am sufficiently brash to think that when I cannot understand particular passages despite all my pains, he himself may not

---

7. Kierkegaard, *Fear and Trembling*, 37.
8. Ibid., 67.
9. Ibid., 112.

have been entirely clear. All this I do easily, naturally, without any mental strain. Thinking about Abraham is another matter, however; then I am shattered. I am constantly aware of the prodigious paradox that is the content of Abraham's life. . . . I *think* myself *into* the hero; I cannot think myself into Abraham.[10]

We begin to see the point. You can be amazed by Abraham, you can even admire him—though you really have to work at it, if you take the story seriously—but you can never, ever "understand" him. At least not here, on Mount Moriah, when the man takes a knife to the throat of his own son.

Significantly, many modern Muslims have tended to find the Akedah far less grotesque than Christians, or Jews for that matter.[11] Obedient faith, they remind us, is hard. Hard, and strange-seeming to the world. It has been a unique feature of the religious landscape of the modern *west* that persons of faith began to reject their religion, and the Book, because the world turned out not to be quite the way they wanted it to be. Kierkegaard understood that extremely well, and faced up to the madness of it—and of faith—as well as anyone. It is likely, in any event, that we are primarily modern Euro-Americans committed to western-style democracy and individual human rights who find this story so grotesque that we nearly have to stop reading it. So we usually ignore it (which is what I am trying to do—and failing). That's precisely the point-of-view Kierkegaard condemned to such devastating effect. But Kierkegaard was crazy in his own way;[12] so if it's really a choice he's offering us, then it's a choice between different forms of madness. That's a problem *Plato* understood best of all.[13]

Barring that deadly sacrifice of his son, abandoned at the last possible moment, the main features of Abraham's character seem more accessible. The grand, overarching metaphors of his life—of wandering,

---

10. Ibid., 32–33.

11. Seyyed Hossein Nasr, a Muslim who left Tehran for the US in 1979, spoke to this very eloquently in a roundtable discussion of the Akedah hosted by Bill Moyers in 1996 and entitled "Genesis: A Living Conversation." Nasr's books include *The Heart of Islam* and *Islam: Religion, History and Civilization*.

12. Kierkegaard says as much at *Fear and Trembling*, 23.

13. Here is how Socrates puts the point at *Phaedrus* 244a: "In fact the best things we have come from madness, when it is given as a gift of the god." He goes on to list among such gifts: prophecy, song, poetry, and erotic love.

patient endurance in the face of endless difficulties, and eventual, perhaps inevitable homecoming—these things resonate just as powerfully in the Hebrew epic as they do in the Greek. Abraham is positively Odyssean in his journeying, though this Hebrew homecoming takes us to a *new* land; it does not return us to an old one. The Hebrew land of Canaan is not like the Greek island of Ithaka, and deep confusion can result from comparing them too superficially. Abraham is ultimately like Cadmus, not Odysseus.

We are back to Jews and Greeks again, back in ways I seem unable to shake. "Hebraism and Hellenism" have been compared by essayists as different in their moral commitments as Ralph Waldo Emerson and Matthew Arnold. Kierkegaard made this comparison central to his analysis of the Akedah, by contrasting Abraham faithfully to the heroism of Greek tragedy. But Kierkegaard was a Christian, whose New Testament forces "Jews and Greeks" into a subtle kind of alignment. It is more interesting to see Philo do so, for he was a Jew, albeit one who wrote and read in Greek.

The classic statement of this cultural and literary dichotomy—of Jews and Greeks—was accomplished by a twentieth century Jew who had been forced to flee Europe, and who wrote his extraordinary book in exile in Istanbul, between 1942 and 1945. Erich Auerbach compared the Akedah to the Homeric rendition of Odysseus's return to Ithaka.[14] Auerbach begins simply by reading the two stories, and he focusses on several of their stranger details. Abraham took three days to reach Mount Moriah with his son. We are not told one word about what he said, or did, or went through in the course of that long journey. Three days—only this. "Three such days," Auerbach writes, "positively demand the symbolic interpretation which they later received," because nearly everything of real importance in this story "remains unexpressed."[15] In other words, the way the Book is written positively *requires* midrash, those later rabbinical commentaries that try to fill in the blanks left by all that the Book so maddeningly fails to say. Everything is rendered in black and white, and most of it is only half-visible, as if concealed in shadow; this accounts for what Auerbach sees as the greater psychological depth and complex-

---

14. *Odyssey* 19:386–469, analyzed in Auerbach, *Mimesis*, 3–26.
15. Auerbach, *Mimesis*, 10–11.

ity of the characters in the Book. We do not really know Abraham at all; perhaps we can't.

Greek characters, by contrast, we know in full. You can imagine a Greek account of those three days *en route* to Mount Moriah. King Agamemnon would surely have had a few choice words for the occasion, railing against the gods' injustice, and the heartache of his own dilemma. Odysseus would have had choicer words of his own, probably would have found some way to lie himself out of the trip, or at least out of the killing. And Athena would have smiled. Greek characters are drawn in color, Auerbach suggests, leaving nothing at all in the shadows, or unexpressed. We know exactly what Greek characters think and feel, because they always tell us (in saying this, Auerbach chooses to ignore the key feature of Odysseus, of course—namely, that he is a masterful liar, an arch-deceiver of friends and gods, alike). There is no past or future tense in Homer, Auerbach suggests, for this reason. There is only a present that is, always, fully present, and rendered in the very clearest light.

There is tremendous insight in this analysis, and it is still more amazing to me that Auerbach managed to conceive it, and to complete it, in exile from most of his own books. But a stunning rejoinder to Auerbach's analysis, anchored in a studied refusal of this very dichotomy—between the Hebraic and Hellenic—is Vassilis Lambropoulos's *The Rise of Eurocentrism*.[16] What Lambropoulos notices is ultimately how unfair these overdrawn categories are to *both* Jews *and* Greeks. It makes Hebrew characters more of a mystery than they ought to be, and overeager child-killers to boot. It turns Greek characters into children, children who cannot grow up because they have no past or future. The analysis ultimately makes nonsense of Odysseus, whose motives are never clear, sometimes not even to himself. Whoever he is, he is not a child. The Hebrew characters fare no better, in Lambropoulos's judgment. For Auerbach's analysis, which erases all the mystery and depth in Odysseus, threatens to make a monster out of Abraham, by claiming that we do not really know if he even feels anything, as clearly he must. In order to make these crude contrasts work, Auerbach has to exaggerate the differences between Greeks and Hebrews to such a degree that he distorts the very stories he is trying to tell. There is a very long history of doing so, Lambropoulos reminds us, of making just this studied Christian contrast, between "Jews" and

---

16. See Lambropoulos, *The Rise of Eurocentrism*, esp. 3–96.

"Greeks." This is how all three "religions of the book," the three scriptural monotheisms, have traditionally dispensed with "paganism," too. So the contrast is ultimately even worse for the Greeks, because they are the ones who get written off most quickly, as "pagan." What I am trying to do in *this* book is to hold these two together, Jews *and* Greeks, admitting their deep differences, but also trying to see how they can mutually inform one another in a larger, perhaps more humane spiritual vision.

Aren't there other ways of talking about these people and their literatures, Lambropoulos asks, ways that stop trying to "compare" Jews and Greeks, and simply let them each be themselves? One of Auerbach's most intriguing contentions is that these differences of literary style, their different ways of "representing reality," result in profoundly different conceptions of the divine—only one of which can be right. How, after all, can you negotiate the difference between monotheism and polytheism? I think that you can, and, as we shall see, I think that Abraham can help. Once we admit that, we may notice other similarities between the Hebraic and the Hellenic, things we missed too quickly and too casually before. Like all the attention to wandering, in both cultures. Both Abraham and Odysseus are *nomads*.[17] And they both embody a characteristically nomadic way of thinking, one that can look surprisingly similar at times. That's been a major theme in *this* book, too.

After that crushing battle with the northern kingdoms, Abraham was no doubt seen as a force to be reckoned with in this, his adoptive land. It was one thing for his God to promise the land to him; it was something else for Abraham to win his place in it through the work of his own wizened, and occasionally warlike, hands. By the end of his life, neighboring kings knew him and treated him with positive deference. They know that everything he touches turns to gold, or else to smoke and ashes.

We do not know a great deal about Sarah's and Abraham's relationship, especially after that awful week when the husband took and nearly killed their son. One wonders how a relationship ever rebounds from a trauma like that. We do know that Abraham essentially did whatever Sarah asked of him, at least within the confines of their home. But then, Abraham *always* does as he is told. When she offered him her hand-

---

17. Lambropoulos has also thought a great deal about such "nomad thought," as is clear in his guest-edited issue of the *South Atlantic Quarterly*, "Ethical Politics"; see especially 849–79. See also "Building Diaspora."

maiden, Hagar, he did as he was told. He conceived a child with her. When Sarah later ordered both mother and child to leave the household, Abraham regretted it, but did nothing to intervene.[18]

We also know that the loss of his beloved wife was a bitter blow to the old man. His grieving is marked in poignant, if subtle, terms—"Avraham set about to lament for Sara and to weep over her"[19]—and a tremendous amount of attention is paid to the acquisition of her burial place. It is one of my favorite glimpses of Abraham at work in this, his adoptive homeland:

> [T]hen Avraham rose from the presence of his dead
> and spoke to the sons of Het, saying:
> I am a sojourner settled among you;
> give me title to a burial holding among you,
> so that I may bury my dead from my presence.
> The sons of Het answered Avraham, saying to him:
> Hear us, my lord!
> You are one exalted by God in our midst—
> in the choicest of our burial-sites you may bury your dead,
> no man among us will deny you his burial-site
> for burying your dead!
> Avraham arose,
> he bowed low to the People of the Land, to the sons of Het,
> and spoke with them, saying:
> If it be then according to your wish
> that I bury my dead from my presence,
> hear me and interpose for me to Efron son of Tzohar,
> that he may give me title to the cave of Makhpela, that is his, that
>   is at the edge of his field,
> for the full silver-worth let him give me title in your midst for a
>   burial holding.
> Now Efron had a seat amidst the sons of Het,
> and Efron the Hittite answered Avraham in the ears of the Sons
>   of Het,

---

18. Gen 16:6–14. A far more critical reading of this strange story is Phyllis Trible's in *Texts of Terror*, 9–35, which bears a closer look for the chilling tales it endeavors to re-tell with more modern moral sensitivities.

19. Gen 23:2.

> of all who had entry to the council-gate of his city,
> saying:
> Not so, my lord, hear me!
> The field I give to you,
> and the cave that is therein, to you I give it;
> before the eyes of the Sons of My People I give it to you—
> bury your dead![20]

Abraham, with whatever combination of self-deprecation and high moral seriousness, describes himself as a simple sojourner among these people (and the Septuagint uses that important word, *paroikos*, again). He is subject to their wishes, and perhaps even subject to their whims. He does not *own* any land here; he always seems to be simply passing through. And for that very reason he is highly vulnerable. Now—and the formality of the setting signals the seriousness of what Abraham is proposing—the foreigner desires to become a land*owner* in this place. The widower claims simply to want a small piece of land in which to bury his wife. But when the sons of Het consent to this, it is clear that they do not consider Abraham a mere sojourner. Not at all. He is a force to be reckoned with, a force to be placated; they treat him with as much deference, if not more, as that which he shows to them.

This is all a wonderful glimpse into the world of tribal niceties, of camel nomads turning with excruciating slowness to landholding. We begin to wonder how they ever got any work done, so busy are they with telling one another how small they are and how great their neighbor is in their eyes. Yet things *are* happening here, just beneath the surface of the story. Abraham is trying to make this as formal an arrangement as he can. He wants to purchase a piece of property; he intends to acquire "title" to it. Later rabbis will make much of the sale of this land for this very reason. And Hebron, the city where this cave-tomb is located, continues to be a singular bone of contention among Palestinians and Israelis for this very reason, to this day.

When Abraham is asked if he has any land in mind, we learn immediately that he most certainly does. He has already scouted out this territory, and has landed upon a cave, which fronts onto a field, that he would very much like to own. He has camped there many times already,

---

20. Gen 23:3–11.

we know.[21] The cave happens to belong to a local Hittite named Efron. And Efron, with a casual wave of his hand, *gives* it to Abraham—not only the cave, but the whole field which lies adjacent to it. He surely knows that Abraham has often been there, and presumably he already knows that Abraham has had his eye on it. So the lovely piece of tense social theater continues:

> Avraham bowed before the People of the Land
> and spoke to Efron in the ears of the People of the Land, saying:
> But if you yourself would only hear me out!
> I will give the silver-payment for the field,
> accept it from me,
> so that I may bury my dead there.
> Efron answered Avraham, saying to him:
> My Lord—hear me!
> A piece of land worth four hundred silver weight,
> what is that between me and you!
> You may bury your dead!
> Avraham hearkened to Efron:
> Avraham weighed out to Efron the silver-worth
> of which he had spoken in the ears of the Sons of Het—
> four hundred silver weight at the going merchants' rate.[22]

Almost without our realizing it, a price has been named, and set, and agreed upon. "A simple field—worth four hundred silver weight, by the way—what is that between you and me?" asks Efron. He has, naturally enough, answered his own question. It is worth, precisely, four hundred weight of silver ("four hundred double-drachmae," says the Septuagint), between himself and God's strange sojourner. No more, and no less. Abraham weighs out the silver before the eyes of the council, and purchases this field with their witness.

> Thus was established the field of Efron, that is in Makhpela, that
>   faces Mamre [*liphnêy Mamre'*],
> the field as well as the cave that is in it, and the trees that were in
>   all the field, that were in all their territory round about,
> for Avraham as an acquisition,

---

21. At Gen 13:18, as we have seen, but most notably at Gen 18:1–2.
22. Gen 23:12–16.

before the eyes of the Sons of Het, of all who had entry to the council-gate of his city.[23]

An interesting translational question emerges just here. Everett Fox translates the Hebrew to imply that the field that Efron sold to Abraham was in a place called Makhpela, and that it *faced* (*liphnêy*) a place called Mamre (that word simply means "the cave").

William Tyndale found this verse somewhat confusing already in 1530; so he assumed that there must have been two caves, and two fields as well. He rendered this passage as follows: "Thus was the field of Ephron wherein the double cave is before Mamre . . ." The Greek Septuagint also turns this into a double cave, *to spêlaion to diploun*,[24] and Philo says that the human body itself resembles such a double cave.[25] The King James translation, which was authorized and completed in 1611, saw something similar at work in this passage, but took a different approach to resolving the complication it presents. The royal translators assumed that there were two *fields*, not two caves: "And the field of Ephron, which *was* in Ma*ch*-pe-läh, which *was* before Mamre, the field . . ." The Revised Standard Version, which was revised yet again in 1991, goes literally and figuratively in a slightly different direction. Here is how they see it and say it: "So the field of Ephron in Machpelah, which was *to the east* of Mamre . . ." We may recall that the Hebrew root, *q-d-m*, has a semantic range that suggests everything from the "east," to the "front," to the "face." This committee of modern translators decided that this semantic connection works in two directions, so that the Hebrew word for face, *p-n(-h)*, may in certain situations also connote "the *east*." If "east" can mean "face," then maybe "face" can mean "east" as well. Naturally, I am intrigued by this eastern possibility, the location of Sarah's somber gravesite "to the east."

East or west, and wherever this cave lay—in a place called Makhpela, or Mamre, or both—this sale of the land brings *her* journey to its completion. Sarah is installed in this newly acquired cave-grave:

---

23. Gen 23:17–18.
24. At Gen 23:9, and then reiterates the point twice at 23:17 and 23:19.
25. Philo *Questions and Answers on Genesis* 4.80.

> Afterward Avraham buried Sara his wife in the cave of the field of Makhpela, facing Mamre [*'al-p'nêy Mamre'*], that is now Hevron,[26] in the land of Canaan.[27]

I have often wondered if Abraham planted a garden near this cave, a floral grave-marker for his dear departed. He did, after all, own the field now, and could presumably do what he wanted with the land. I like to think he did. But gardens, be sure to recall, have a funny way of blurring borders rather than ensuring them. And therein lies a tale.

---

26. It is worth noticing that this second, more modern, name of the site (*Hevrôn*) sounds more than a little like the name of the Hittite to whom it had once belonged (*'Efrôn*).

27. Gen 23:19.

chapter nine

GENERATION

Secularism, I suspect, is a pretense; at the very least it is an artificial attempt to dualistically divide a holistic world. Institutions, humanistic or not, are sometimes sarcophagi, petrified flesh eaters, hiding from us the religious character of experience. But religion is made of stories, of myths and dreams, which seep out of institutions and animate whatever their breath brushes....

Having forgotten or rejected the traditional texts, we must fabricate, make up our sacred stories as we go along. If the traditional story of the Fall now reverberates with dualism and its sexist and anti-ecological subcategories, and yet our personal memories keep insinuating the same old images even though we have neglected the old story, what shall we do? Medieval travelers tried, by means of geography, theology, and imagination, to find their way back to Paradise. The contemporary imagination no longer seeks that prelapsarian womb; if we make the journey to Paradise, we want to look over its walls and glimpse the Garden after the Fall.[1]

...

It is mid-afternoon now, and I am beginning to get hungry. The sun is coyly peeking out from behind an ornate curtain of puffy cloud. It

---

1. Sexson, *Ordinarily Sacred*, 55, 126.

is almost beginning to feel like summer again, that wonderful "Indian summer," southern-style, the kind we come to expect at this time of the year in this locale. It will be "summer" again tomorrow; I can feel it. The green is still brilliant against the recollected grey of early morning, and the ground is no longer damp. It feels a bit steamy, as the last vestiges of raindrop moisture flee the ground for the sky. And the gardener is for a latish lunch. One never tires of the taste of fresh tomatoes, not now, not when you know that they will only be available for two or three weeks more, at the most. Time, then, for an afternoon repast . . . another tomato sandwich, despite the fact that I've already eaten one today.

One thing that has always impressed me about the diet of the eastern Mediterranean is its fairly limited repertoire of forms. I am convinced that this entire eastern Mediterranean world, from Greece and Italy in the west, Cyprus and Turkey to the north, the north African coast of Egypt, Libya and Tunisia to the south, and the Palestinian/Israeli coast (as you have surely thought to notice by now) to the east . . . *this entire world shares a common culture*, despite the local varieties of flora, fauna, and cuisine.[2] I suspect that the eastern Mediterranean has been linked this way for millennia. There is a fascinating early Bronze Age shipwreck off the southern coast of Turkey, just west of Antalya—in between the Turkish port of Kaş and the Greek island of Kastellorizo across the channel (this is where the Italian film "Mediterraneo" was filmed, some years ago). The site was excavated by a North American team of underwater archaeologists in the 1980s. Judging on the basis of its cargo, which survived virtually intact and at great depth, it seems as if this ship really did not have a home port in the modern sense, but rather endlessly plied these selfsame eastern waters: from Greece and the Aegean islands, to Crete, along the coasts of North Africa and Israel, back to Cyprus, and southern Turkey, where it eventually sank. Each of these port towns was linked via overland trade-routes and caravansaries to still more distant arenas of trade; there was lapis lazuli from *Afghanistan* on board the wreck, for instance. And this was all 3500 years ago . . .[3] Culinary and

2. Anyone who feels for the Mediterranean as I do will simply revel in the words and images of Predrag Matvejevich's luminous book, *Mediterranean: A Cultural Landscape*.

3. A wonderful archaeological report of these findings, written by U.S. archaeologist George Bass, is entitled "Oldest Known Shipwreck Reveals Bronze Age Splendors." The wreck itself has been reconstructed in a lovely maritime museum in a Venetian fortress in the Turkish harbor of Bodrum.

cultural similarity, if not quite sameness, has always been the hallmark of this central-seeming and mixed-up Sea.

One tends to eat the same things at the same times of the day throughout this part of the world. There is variety, to be sure, especially closer to the coasts, but it is more like the variation one meets in musicians who play the same pieces of music. They play, as I say, within a surprisingly limited repertoire of forms, or notes, or (in this case) raw foodstuffs. One of the Mediterranean's finest, most subtle and enthusiastic aficionados who wrote in English in the last century was Lawrence Durrell. He spent two definitive years in Corfu prior to the Second World War; after spending six months there myself, I begin to understand how it might have changed him.[4] Durrell extends my borders a bit, including the *western* Mediterranean as well as the eastern half in his descriptions. For Durrell settled ultimately in southern France, in the Midi.[5] Here, in any event, is what Durrell noticed, heading south through the Provence, heading homeward, toward that Sea. Durrell knows himself to be "home," simply by attending carefully to what his neighbors are eating:

> Here the Mediterranean begins [!] with its characteristic cuisine based on garlic and olive oil, its concentration on herbs—saffron, thyme, fennel, sage, black pepper. Here, too, the apéretif changes to *pastis*—an aniseed drink which is a mild second cousin to the brain-storming northern Pernod. This, too, is the territory in which you make your first tentative exploration of the little rosé wines which are hardly known abroad. Under the dusty glare of Provençal sunlight the new diet seems supremely appropriate; appropriate too that the accents begin to change from chicken and mutton to fish—which comes to its apotheosis in the great *bouillabaisse* cauldrons of the port of Marseilles! . . . Provence! The new world is a pre-Christian one, with its mouldering monuments of the Roman occupation, its sculptured reliefs and shattered columns; even the bullfights you will see in the ancient arenas of Arles and Nimes will remind you that the parentage of this ancient ritual goes back to Crete and is pictured on the Minoan vases.[6]

---

4. The book it later inspired, *Prospero's Cell: A Guide to the Landscape and Manners of the Island of Corfu*, is still one of his best.

5. For more on this geographical movement, see my essay, "By the Waters of Delphi." Durrell devoted his last book to the Provence, a marvelous thing entitled *Caesar's Vast Ghost: Aspects of Provence*, with photographs by Harry Peccinotti.

6. Durrell, *Spirit of Place*, 330–31.

Unthinkable as it seems to eat anything other than tomatoes in the Mediterranean summer, they are in fact a New World fruit, and thus were unknown in antiquity. Socrates would never have tasted one, nor would he ever have smoked a cigarette, nor eaten a potato.[7] (That said, by the second decade of the nineteenth century, the storied Vatican gardens boasted several kinds of tobacco plants, which they choreographed as a sort of exotic ornamental. They tended enormous vineyards as well. But no tomatoes, so far as I can tell.[8])

The tomato hails originally from the coastal highlands of Equador, Peru, and Chile. It was the Spanish who exported it to the Mediterranean basin, where it exploded, literally and figuratively, on those seaside palates. Well established in southern France, if not in England, it made its transatlantic way back to North America—ironically enough, coming there from Europe in the *east*, not from the Andean highlands to the *south*. Thomas Jefferson's garden diaries indicate that he was already cultivating tomatoes as early as 1809 at Monticello, despite the fact that many of his neighbors thought them poisonous.[9] From the Andes, to the Mediterranean, to the blue hills of Virginia . . . the modern circuit of trade exceeds even the ancient Mediterranean one visible at Kaş.

Eating tomatoes twice, or thrice, daily is a quiet, emphatically *local*, pleasure. It ironically reminds me of another, a more eastern, world. Strangely, I think of the tomato as a Mediterranean fruit, not a New World one. And there is no monotony in the face of its spectacular nuances of taste, and the subtlety of its flavors when it is fresh. I pinch off a few sprigs of basil, one dark red tomato, and bring them inside to place on fresh bread, still slightly warm from the oven, accompanied by a wedge of feta cheese. Wonderful.

It was my grandfather who taught me to relish such simple things, years ago, in *his* garden. I had never heard of a tomato sandwich, much less envisioned eating such a thing, until one auspicious, especially hot summer day in his kitchen. I had been working all morning in the woodshop he installed in his basement; he had come home from work so that

---

7. Durrell makes much of these facts in his *Sicilian Carousel*, 64–67. For more on the astonishing variety of New World imports, and the way they changed the culture of the Old, the interested will profit from a look at Anthony Grafton's *New Worlds, Ancient Texts*, esp. 161–93.

8. Abundant records of these gardens may be found in the "Secret Archives" of the Vatican Library (Archivio Segreto Vaticano, or ASV): S.P.A. *Titoli* 101, fasc. 1.

9. See Simon, *Dear Mr. Jefferson*, 14–16.

we might have lunch together. His garden was always heavy-laden with the most impressive beefsteak tomatoes in those steamy summer months in New Jersey. He suggested cutting one up, served on thick dark bread with a dollop of mayonnaise. Eyebrows arched, I consented, putting on the water for tea. But within the hour, I was a convert. Still later—after I'd excavated in Crete for six years, and lived in Athens for two more—I learned to add basil, then feta, to the mixture. Improving on imported traditions, with the help of fresh local fare. That is virtually an arch-metaphor for the Book.

My grandfather, J. Thomas Holt, helped me to build the enormous wooden desk upon which I am attempting to order this jumbled clutter of biblical and horticultural musings today. He helped me to build many things, as he helped me to see and to understand many more. When he passed away in the bitter winter cold of late-January 1989, on the execrable thirteenth of the month, I came into possession of several artifacts that are still among my most prized possessions: a lovely old Hamilton wristwatch, given to him by his company as a Christmas gift in 1929 (no doubt ordered before, and presented after, the great Stock Market Crash of that grim October);[10] a pretty gold pocket watch that I rarely have the opportunity to wear, fashion today being what it is (or isn't); and two small artifacts from his own boyhood on a Maryland farm. First, there is a bizarre, over-large file that they used to cut the teeth of the horses, which can become dangerously sharp from the constant abrasion of the grains they normally eat. I still haven't come up with any very good idea for how to use the thing, but I can't bear to part with it. Second, there is an oddly curved wooden stick with a natural sort of a handle that he used to poke holes in the freshly plowed soil, for planting. I still use this one, on rare occasions, in *my* garden. Just to maintain the contact.

Grandfather was raised on a farm at the head of the Chesapeake Bay—in Maryland, shortly before the turn of the century. He was born in 1898. The times being what they were—namely, hopelessly *under*developed, by comparison with our modern lives and times—his father owned one hundred acres of farmland with one full mile of waterfront on the Bay. His father's brother owned the adjacent hundred acres, and his eldest brother bought the hundred-acre plot to the east. Three hundred acres of

---

10. In a bizarre twist of fate, this same watch was stolen in New York City on another brutally cold January day, just one day before his daughter, my mother, passed on in her own artful and elegant way. I find it difficult to describe the painfulness, yet also the poignancy, of this: that things, *precious* things, so often do not last.

land, with fully three miles of riverfront: it would be worth an unthinkable fortune today. I wonder what sort of Hittite they initially bought it from.

My great-grandfather was known to be a bit tight with his wallet. And Grandfather was his youngest son. After the departure of all the others, the father seemed committed to giving the farm a go for several seasons more, just for the money—with my grandfather doing the lion's share of the work, of course. Grandfather was, naturally, less keen on the idea. So he ran away from home at the age of fourteen. He landed on his feet in Coatesville, Pennsylvania, amidst the impossible fertility and vast rolling beauty of Lancaster County, where the Amish are settled now. He found work—not on a farm (he had doubtless tired of that line of work)—but as an armature-winder at one of the local electric motor assembly-plants. Apparently, the foreman took a liking to this gangly fifteen-year-old, and taught him all about being a mechanic, which Grandfather became, for the larger part of his ninety-year sojourn among us. He worked in construction, mostly, and I often marvel at the transformations of the northeast corridor of this country that he witnessed in the course of his long life—not to mention how many of these changes for which he was himself responsible. I have a picture of him at age fifty—the time in a man's life when, as Voltaire put it, he finally wears the face that he has earned. I take great comfort in the quiet serenity of my Grandfather's face in the fullness of his age.

J. Thomas Holt (November 22, 1898–January 13, 1989)

He worked on bridges, skyscrapers, a whole slew of military barracks and temporary camps when the wars of mid-century came on, and other things, tirelessly repairing the heavy equipment that helped bring all these things into being. He met my grandmother in Coatesville some years later. He married her in time, then the couple set out again for the greener pastures of New Jersey, where he started up the construction machinery company that still bears his name. It was there in any case, in New Jersey, that my mother and father were both born and raised. And it was from that state that *I* fled, at my earliest opportunity, heading back south again, toward what (I was convinced) were greener pastures, and certainly warmer ones—taking up my collegiate studies in North Carolina. I actually passed very near to Grandfather's household farm, just to get where I was going, although I didn't realize this at the time. That happened fairly regularly to the biblical patriarchs, too, now that I think on it; even when we move independently and of our own volition, we are still unwittingly retracing someone else's steps. Our steps can seem strangely foreordained whether we are moving toward a goal, or merely wandering. Not all who wander are lost. The frontier is perhaps as much a fiction as a fact.

Grandfather's wife departed this life in 1978, the year before I departed for college. Grandfather survived her for nearly a decade; he died just one month before I left the country for that two-year sojourn in Greece I have mentioned obliquely several times before. The couple are both buried in a small family plot in Coatesville, up on a hill overlooking the river where they courted nearly a century ago. It is bitterly cold there in the winter, depressingly wet in the fall, but oh, the heartbreaking beauty of the place in the rich, full bloom of late spring and early summer. I have always liked it there; it's one of the few things about the northeast I truly miss. My mother's gravesite is another.

In between 1978 and 1989, Grandfather continued to do most of the things he'd always done. He remained in the home where he and my grandmother lost their first child, then raised two boys and my mother to adulthood. He worked, nearly every day. He took brief vacations—to Atlantic City and Las Vegas, mostly—normally in the company of his sons. But later in life, he started traveling more, taking more time off, and he started doing the one thing I'd never have picked him for in a million years. He started going to Florida—just like every other sunbelt retiree I'd ever known or heard about. But Grandfather hadn't retired.

The fact of the matter is that Grandfather had put away his mourning after an appropriate time—had decided, in the biblical idiom I especially love, to "gird up his loins and walk among his people again."[11] Grandfather had met another woman with whom he enjoyed spending his freer time. It was a complicated matter for his children, I'm sure—less so for his grandchildren, who simply liked the very apparent fact that he was happy. And it was oddly difficult to talk about. I chuckle now to recall how we all went out of our way to refer to her as Grandfather's "traveling companion." Even when *he* was traveling, alone, to see *her* . . .

One of the many things I learned from my Grandfather, long before I'd begun reading these stories in the Book, is the sheer enormity, but also the sheer human poignancy, of learning how to begin again. I learned this from Grandfather better, and earlier, than I did from the Book. It makes a difference as well that Grandfather was a gardener; in the face of a life he still had to live, he opted to live it, and to live it abundantly. He did so in the happy company of countless others who so obviously admired him. He was a remarkable man, graced with one of the most beautiful and singular souls it's ever been my rare privilege to know and grow to love. And I feel heartened, vaguely comforted somehow, to know that he did not travel those later years alone.

When Sarah died, Abraham was an old man himself—if she was one hundred and twenty-seven,[12] then he was roughly one hundred and thirty-six. We are told that Sarah was ninety years old when God reiterated the covenant and changed her name.[13] At that same time, Abraham was ninety-nine.[14] So there were roughly nine years between them. Amazingly, however, *Abraham married again*—a local woman named Keturah, this time, and he had lots of children with her. She was different in every way from Sarah—fertile and abundant, not sparing, the child of a different generation and, more significantly still, the child of a different place. She was *from* the land of Canaan. The Book mentions six sons that Keturah bore to Abraham, and traces the subsequent generations of two of them,

---

11. A phrase loosely borrowed from 2 Sam 19:1–8 and Job 38:3, 40:7.
12. Gen 23:1.
13. Gen 17:17.
14. Gen17:1.

paying special attention to the tribes that took their names. Some later rabbinic traditions suggest that these men settled south, in the Arabian Peninsula as well. This gives further warrant to the Qur'an's assertion of a closer connection to Abraham, the proverbial "father of *many* nations." It also serves to remind me of why I picked up the Book in the first place, in that faraway September six autumns ago. I had hoped to learn from it who we, and others, are. But of course, the Book does not answer questions like that. It simply puts the problem for us.

Abraham's eldest son was conceived with a woman not his first wife. And we will remember that, jealous as Sarah became of both Hagar and Ishmael, Abraham continued to show deep concern for them both. Yet it was Isaac, the younger son, the one he nearly killed, who became the proverbial apple in his father's eye. All of these children now presented an acute problem of inheritance. The Book resolves it for us in characteristic fashion—in the east. To Isaac, we are told, Abraham gave all that he owned. But he did not forget his impressive brood of later sons.

> But Avraham gave over all that was his to Yitzhak.
> And to the sons of the concubines that Avraham had, Avraham
>   gave gifts, and he sent them away from Yitzhak his son
> while he was still alive, eastward, to the Eastland [*qêdmah 'el-
>   'eretz qedem*].[15]

The east is mentioned twice here—"east to the Eastland"—doubled, as if for emphasis (this is true in the Septuagint's Greek as well, *pros anatolas eis gên anatolôn*). So these petty and not-so-petty biblical problems are normally resolved—with separation and migration, migration always, so it would seem, to the east.

And with this last, long, poignantly eastward-looking movement, the story of Abraham comes to an end. In a foreign place.

> A hundred years and seventy years and five years, then he
>   expired.
> Avraham died at a good ripe-age, old and satisfied (in days),
> and was gathered to his kinspeople.

---

15. Gen 25:5–6.

> Yitzhak and Yishmael his sons buried him, in the cave of
> > Makhpela, in the field of Efron son of Tzohar the Hittite, that
> > faces Mamre ['al-p'nêy Mamre'],[16]
> the field that Avraham had acquired from the sons of Het.
> There were buried Avraham and Sara his wife.[17]

So Abraham's long sojourn on the earth comes to its quiet and fairly *un*dramatic conclusion, at least by modern movie-going standards. He has been a rich character, but also a highly mysterious one. An actively religious man who conversed openly, and even controversially, with his God, he was capable of jarringly swift and decisive life-decisions, of putting his life and the lives of those around him repeatedly on the line. He was capable of a singular, and almost terrifying, obedience. He exceeds even the Phoenician-Greek called Cadmus in this. Recalling Adam's gift with words, and their responsibilities, Abraham renamed many places through which he passed, proclaiming his God in that way, too. And so he transformed the physical, as well as the religious, landscape of Canaan. He dug wells, raised altars, offered sacrifices and testimonies to his God—and everywhere, absolutely everywhere, he prospered. He lived to see all of his sons grown true and strong, many of them with children of their own. And he was laid to his rest by the doting hands of his two eldest sons, "gathered," so the Hebrew has it, "to his kinspeople."

I am especially struck by Abraham's obedience to the very first divine command he ever heard: the one that commanded him to leave his home, and to live out the rest of his life as a resident alien—an alien, as things turned out, in the west. When Abraham's long life of almost continual wandering comes to an end, he is laid to rest in a little plot of *western* ground that about-faces onto the field from which it takes it name, Makhpela near Mamre—*to the east*. In death, then, Abraham and his wife face the rising sun each morning, the sun that wanders on its way to them from the direction of their former home, in the east. And yet we are led to feel that Abraham has come *home*, somehow, at the last, home to a small piece of especially well-loved ground that he had made his very own. He lies buried in what seemed to be his very favorite spot while

---

16. Remember that this same phrase has also been translated as "facing east of Mamre." And here once again, the Septuagint refers to it as a "double cave" (*to spêlaion to diploun*).

17. Gen 25:8–10.

he sojourned here, his favorite campground now become a final resting-place for him and his first wife. He has come home, as we are invited to recognize all of humanity doing—home from the east, where we were all first exiled, from a Garden.

chapter ten

SLEEP

The mind of the serious man is a sojourner [*paroikos*] in its bodily place rather than an inhabitant [*katoikos*] there. For his fatherland is the ether, and heaven.[1]

...

"And the Lord said to Abraham: 'Go out of your land, and away from your kin, and out of your father's house, and into the land that I will show you...'" (Gen 12:1)

...

God's work of cleansing the human soul begins by providing it with an escape from out of three countries and into complete salvation. The three countries are body [*sômatos*], sense-perception [*aisthêseôs*], and speech [*logou*]. "The land" is a symbol for the body, "kin" are a symbol of sense-perception, and "father's house" is a symbol of speech. How so? you may ask...[2]

...

Twilight now, whose unexpected and surprisingly early arrival speaks to the sudden onset of autumn. The last dappled spots of sunlight filter through the leaves that are still green, but darkening. There is a damp

---

1. Philo *Questions and Answers on Genesis* 3.45.
2. Philo *The Migration of Abraham* [436] 1–2.

chill in the air now toward dusk, not due to the rains this time, rather due simply to the natural fact of seasonal oscillation and change. It is mid-October—and nearly the birthday of the world, according to old Bishop Ussher—the shadows lengthening now, and one can almost feel it, the sheer anxiety that must have greeted this season in antiquity. Some last green tomatoes are clinging to the mostly brown and withered vines, trying manfully to turn. The cold-weather crops—the lettuces and brussel sprouts, the various greens and parsleys, the broccoli and cauliflower and garden beans—these may hold out for two months or more, if the weather does. And a precious few of them, like the cabbages, will stay fresh all winter long, barring some sort of natural disaster. Still, in the past people must have wondered—in an age without refrigeration, with so many hard-working mouths to feed, with significant flocks to feed as well, and with substantially more limited resources—if they had put enough food away in the summertime to survive the cold that they felt coming. Famine—that awful fate of most ancient peoples, and the sometime-bane of modern life as well—drove Abraham south into Egypt once.[3] It drove his son to the land of Gerar, halfway to Egypt,[4] and it was destined to drive his grandson and all of his great-grandchildren to Egypt, yet again, for over four hundred years.[5]

Human hopefulness being what it is, most agricultural societies greet this autumnal anxiety with operatic flamboyance. They throw a party. This autumn party is one, moreover, in which we waste the very resources we ought to be hoarding most jealously. We eat the last of the fresh produce, test out the new wine, and invite a temporary forgetfulness. I have always especially loved these harvest festivals. So did the Hebrew God, apparently, who instituted at least two of them: when the first fruits are in-gathered; and then again when the late crops—like olives and figs and grapes—are harvested at the last.[6]

I did not do much in the garden after my mid-afternoon lunch. There is less and less to do now, save putting the various garden-spaces to bed for a fine, fallow sleep of their own. So I took a leisurely nap myself, while

---

3. Gen 12:10—13:1.
4. Gen 26:1–33.
5. Gen 41:53—47:13.
6. Exod 23:14–17.

the sun played peek-a-boo behind a constantly shifting wall of dappled clouds. Arisen now with a cup of coffee—the third, smiling cup of the day—I am shaking the sleep out of still-tired limbs, walking the length and breadth of my own little plot, reveling in the spectacular hues with which late-afternoon sunshine paints the puffy clouds in the west, nearer to the day's more sudden and ever-more-dramatic autumnal endings.

Viewed with the eyes of an archaeologist, this place has real interest. The garden lies atop what must once have been the foundation of a *very* large home, a home such as the ones that still stand to the right and left of me. But that home burned down more than seventy years ago, I am told, and the second house (a largish servant's cottage, most likely) to the rear of the property burned down well over a decade ago. This devastating conflagration gave birth to "Kamp Karma," the modernist home my first landlady built on this same plot, the one in which I was a resident sojourner for several years. Each extension of the garden has turned up a virtual treasure trove of Atlantan antiquities—mostly brick, from what appear to have been the massive fireplaces and foundations on which the original house stood. I have excavated enough brick here in the last ten years to line the entire garden with them, as well as several flower-beds to the front and sides of my second home. I have also come across the occasional antique bottle, charred pieces of wood, other things whose stories would need someone with greater imagination, and a more acute poetic eye, than I possess to be told properly. Still and all, the land here has great interest, each and every time I work it.

I am standing to the west of the garden now, facing east. It is the best spot from which to survey the entire business in the waning last light of day. This position also just so happens to put me in view of a striking piece of gorgeous pink marble for which Georgia is justly famous. It is a simple, single rectangular slab which has been here far longer than I have been, judging by the mottling and casual overgrowth, and it bears a single name, inscribed on two sides of the stone: "DR. BARKER."

Dr. Barker's hitching post

I assume it was a hitching post of sorts, something to which he'd tie the team that took him by carriage to work each day in the downtown area nearby. Several years ago, I devoted several months in the late fall at various state archives—in Atlanta, and Raleigh, and Birmingham, and Knoxville, and Nashville—looking for some further sign of the man. Eventually, I found him. His story will seem eerily familiar, almost predestinate in places, to anyone who has made their way this far in mine.

His name was Novatus Lee Barker. A curious namesake, it is borrowed from the famous Roman Stoic philosopher, Seneca the Younger, whose brother was named Novatus, until he took the name of his patron in Greece: Junius Gallio. It was with this second name that he appears in the Christian New Testament,[7] as the local Roman governor before whom the Jews of Corinth unsuccessfully tried to get Paul prosecuted and later jailed.

The modern Novatus's parents (Sarah Claywell Eidson and Thomas Arthur Barker) hailed from the east—more specifically from North Carolina, and more specifically still, from the lake area north of Charlotte. It's easy to lose sight of just how long the city of Atlanta has served as both a clearinghouse and a gateway for all the states and counties around her: Mississippi and Alabama, to the west; Tennessee and Kentucky, to the north; North and South Carolina, to the east; even Florida, to a lesser degree, further to the south. His parents departed the Carolinas shortly

---

7. Acts 18:12–17.

after their marriage in 1849, when Thomas found work on the new railroad then being built outside of Atlanta. Thus their son, Novatus, was born in Troup County, Georgia, on the 24th of May, 1864—not so very long before Union troops under General William Tecumseh Sherman burned Atlanta to the ground, destroying whatever record of the couple's (or their son's) arrival I might otherwise have been able to secure.

Novatus Lee was the fifth of six children, and several of his siblings sported names every bit as unusual as his own. I am struck especially by two of the brothers: Euschius Zephaniah, born in 1853; and Lionius Eugene, born in 1854. The other siblings had less memorable names: Marion, born in 1850; Mildred, born in 1854; and Thomas Eugene, born quite a bit later, in 1869.

Novatus Lee Barker appears suddenly in his own right on the U.S. Census in 1900, where he is recorded as living in West Point, Georgia, a thriving city very near the Alabama border and not far from where he was born.[8] The city's name really seems to tell a tale, despite historians' insistence that it is not so. The town marked the western terminus of the Atlanta and West Point Railroad, whose lines Novatus's father helped to lay between 1848 and 1854 (amazingly, another railroad linking West Point to Montgomery had already been completed). So it was that a site first intended in the 1820s as a trading post for the indigenous peoples densely settled on the western side of the Chattahoochee River, later became a largish milltown in which western Georgians turned all of that Alabama cotton into new clothing, then shipped it away. The town was called Franklin originally, but was incorporated as West Point in 1832, well before the railroads came (the town boasted fewer than two hundred souls back then, and there was already a larger city named Franklin nearby—hence the name-change). The town was pretty thoroughly destroyed in 1865 by Union troops; they even cut the bridge spanning the river here, an act the locals referred to ever after as an act of "vandalism" rather than an act of war. And so the citizens of West Point did what most of the characters in this book have done: they began all over again.

Novatus's first wife was named Mary Lyon, though she went by Mary H. after their marriage. She was from this area as well, and so the

---

8. A superb reference work on this area is Clifford L. Smith's *History of Troup County*, esp. 54–57. It is interesting to note that Novatus L. Barker, *Junior*, a veteran of the First World War, is acknowledged at the beginning of this book as City Clerk of West Point, Georgia, a post he took up in 1927.

couple remained there. Novatus was a Dry Goods merchant who ran "Barker's Bargain House" and owned his own home, free of any mortgage obligations—which was perhaps not so unusual in that more frugal and cautious time.

Barker's dry goods store

The home of Novatus Lee Barker

His entire life will speak to this same tireless spirit of responsibility, steadfastness (even when he is wandering), and an almost Stoic sense of domestic duty. Mary bore him a son in their first year together, Novatus Jr., who lived out his own adult life in West Point as well. He would serve as Fire Chief, City Clerk, and City Recorder for nearly fifty years, from 1927 until his death in 1974, and he is buried in a separate family plot, with his wife, Ethel Johnson, who joined him in the way of all earth just two years later.

A second son was born to Novatus the elder and Mary just three years later. They named him George Lyon Barker; he died within nine months. This was a major trauma in the father's early married life, I suspect. For seventeen years later, and married to a second wife by then, that lost child was clearly still on his mind. He named yet *another* one of his sons George—George Croft Barker, this time—selecting his second wife's maiden name for the child, just as he had done for the doomed infant, two decades before. One can only speculate over what he thought and felt while doing so a second time. In any event, that child survived to adulthood, had a son of his own in turn (George Croft Jr.), and died in 1997. His remains are installed next to those of his father and mother.

Mary Barker "passed unto our Father's house" on the 18th of June, 1903, after thirteen luckless years of marriage. Her headstone tells her story with a somber eloquence: "An unpretentious Christian character / she professed little, but like Christ / she wrought more than she talked." A silent woman, a dutiful wife, called home much too soon. She dies, and just as quickly, she disappears. The widower took a younger woman to wife on August 12th of the very next year: He married Miss Lillian Croft, whose family hailed from across the river, in neighboring Chambers County, Alabama. The new couple would dance back and forth across that border for the next fifteen years, until they finally cast their fortunes on Atlanta. One might say in retrospect that it was a mistaken choice, this fateful and Lot-like return to the eastland—though they couldn't have known that at the time. No one can evaluate such decisions, in the end.

They had six children together, evenly spaced, one born every two years or so: Mildred (1905), Gwendolyn (1907), Marion (1909) and George (1911), all born in Georgia; Thomas (1913) and Lillian (1916) were both born in Alabama. The growing family sat out the Great War in Alabama; only Novatus Jr. served with distinction in Europe. Meanwhile, Novatus the elder devoted himself to his studies. The land on which their house would eventually stand (and where my garden grows now) was a vacant lot until a man named Chestnut built on it at the end of the War. That happened in 1918. In 1918, the Atlanta City Directory still advertised local chapters of the Ku Klux Klan, right next to the Knights of Columbus. In 1918, none of the Barkers lived permanently in Georgia. In 1919, everything changed.

For the elder Novatus had elected to change careers at mid-life. In the words of his 1917 Class Yearbook, *The Aesculapian*, "thinking that such a personage as his should not be thus restrained, [he] launched his submarine in the medical sea as a full-fledged Freshman in 1913."[9] He had apparently already trained at the Weltner Institute of Suggestive Therapeutics in Missouri, and later continued his residential training in New York and Atlanta. He graduated from Emory University (my *alma mater* too, where I was destined to become a very different kind of doctor) as a trained neurologist, and his graduation photograph contributes an important dimension to his story.

A handsome man with a stern and serious face, thin set lips and a firm jaw, he looks very much like his president, Woodrow Wilson, celebrated for traits of character eerily similar to the good doctor's. The motto chosen for him by his classmates confirms this: "Truth and honesty fear no man."[10]

Novatus Lee Barker settled permanently in Atlanta without his family in 1919; alas, there were fewer Barkers to resettle. The couple's eldest child, Mildred Eidson, died on January 14th, 1919, at the outset of a devastating influenza plague which took more lives in two years than a world

---

9. The 1917 yearbook made naval imagery central to its presentation of the graduating class. So at the outset of the Senior Class History:

> On the fateful morning of September 29, 1913, the good ship "Class of Seventeen" set sail upon the azure deep of Emory University Medical School on a far-destined journey in search of that modern golden fleece, an M.D. degree. Our crew numbered seventy-seven of the hardiest jackies that ever manned a boat. All went well for the first era of our voyage, as each sailor learned more of the duties aboard the Argosy and caught the spirit of the trip, friendship and study.

10. The Senior Class "prophecy" confirms the respectful distance most gave to him:

> Daddy Barker, who after many years of successful experience in psychotherapy, has succeeded in convincing the Faculty of the A.M.C. of the desirability of such a department, and is now filling that chair with distinction and honour.

Novatus Lee Barker (May 24, 1864–January 9, 1944)

war had taken in four. The child took ill on January 9th, and gave up the ghost shortly after midnight on the 14th. I can't help recalling that a similar experience at this same time nearly broke the spirit of Sigmund Freud, who lost a daughter to this same plague. Freud wrote what is without a doubt his strangest book, *Beyond the Pleasure Principle*, by way of coping with the loss. Novatus, also a psychologist, simply pressed on.

He was already fifty-three years old when he changed careers (his classmates called him "Kid" Barker, as a joke, though they also called him "Daddy"), and he set up his shingle downtown, working on Peachtree Street until finally giving up on Atlanta in 1932. He lived out that first year in the Vernon Apartments on—I'm not making any of this up—*East Cain*. And in the very next year, the 1920 U.S. Census locates Novatus and the entire Barker family here, on *this* land, in *that* lost house. The times being what they were, the family also employed a cook who lived with them, a twenty-four-year-old widow of African and Georgian descent named Lillian Harris. And next door to them, in the same house where I am reconstructing their story now, lived a considerably smaller family: Mr. Linton K. Starr, his wife Sarah, and their six-year-old daughter, also sporting the then-popular name of Lillian. That couple stayed here, in this house, long after the Barkers lost theirs. Mrs. Starr hung on here until 1942, in fact.

The house where I am living now provides some sense of how the Barkers must have lived then. My house has been divided into four large apartments, in which as many as eleven people have lived quite comfortably; in 1930, it was worth $20,000.00. The Barkers' property next door was worth nearly twice that. By 1923, they already had their first boarder. In 1925, there were four, and in the 1926 Atlanta City Directory these apartments are listed as a separate building with a separate (half)address. In 1927, that address contained nine apartments in total, all of them occupied. (They lived across the street from a boarding house in West Point, so they knew the business well).

Then tragedy's bell struck, as it often does, three times. The Barkers' home burned to the ground in 1931; the lot was listed as vacant, once again, in the 1933 City Directory. It was also in 1930, the Depression now a permanent feature of American cultural and economic life, that Novatus lost his second wife, Lillian, who slowly gave out after a two-and-a-half-year battle with uterine and cervical cancer. She died in the early hours of September 25th, and was buried the very next day in West Point. So the disasters multiplied: Stock Market Crash, Great Depression, the loss of a well-loved wife, the loss of their home—a shattering time. Novatus tried to keep it going in Atlanta for a while, holding out against Depression, and personal grief. He worked one last year downtown, left his practice, and slowly watched his boarders move away. This patriarch's extended household dwindled away to nearly nothing. Five apartments out of nine were empty in 1931, six of them in 1932; only Mrs. Eulah Miles still lived with the aging widower by 1933.

He clearly could have made a go of it here, since whoever bought this lot from him had successfully rented out all but one apartment in 1934. No, Novatus Lee Barker had simply run out of steam, or at least run out of the heart and stomach for Atlanta. So he left. He continued to practice in Eastman, about one hundred miles south of Atlanta, for a while. But he finally retired in 1940, as the country geared up for yet another war. Newly retired, twice widowed, and exhausted with the long labors of beginning so often again, he turned to another "home" of sorts. He went north, this time, rounding out his days in Knoxville, Tennessee, where his second daughter, Gwendolyn, lived with her husband, T. L. Hollingsworth Jr. Novatus battled with congestive heart trouble, and epilepsy—an especially cruel fate for a psychotherapist—and he began to fail seriously in his final year, rounding out his days during an unusually cold winter in the Tennessee River Valley, very far from home.

But he is not buried there. In the purest sense, Novatus Lee Barker returned to the west, back to West Point, back to its pretty rivers and quiet lakes, back to that glorious green that graces her fields and hills all year round. Novatus Lee Barker departed this earth on January 19, 1944, just as the war in Europe began swinging the Allies' way. I like it that his life, so often sour, may have ended on a sweet note.

I located his grave on a brilliantly sunny Sunday afternoon, on an early October morning that still felt like July. The trip itself was emblematically southern, poignant and epic. Long stretches of green highway, sunlight glinting through a poetic umbrella of thick kudzu, dying forest, and late afternoon light. Long stretches of utterly undeveloped territory southwest of Atlanta, driving through the vast silences of history: the old White House with its attendant hot-springs, where Franklin Roosevelt died, not long after Novatus Barker did; redneck and peckerwood towns withering on the interstate vine, with names that recall the languages of the indigenous peoples as often as they do Homeric poems or Roman history; the glorious if indistinct southern revelry in summer past its time. When I left the highway, I traveled along a local route that is named after Dr. Martin Luther King Jr. now. And when I stopped at a local church for directions to the old Pinewood Cemetery, a smiling, sweat-beaded congregant happily informed me that I was only a block away. It took no more than forty-five minutes to locate the Barker family plot (both of them, in fact) and I sat on a pretty, low bench they'd placed there, meditating on the stones and the stories they were trying to tell. I left some flowers I'd picked from their old home, and took away a small piece of chipped marble to place on top of Dr. Barker's hitching-post at mine. By the time I got back home, it was raining and very much colder. In the east.

When the patriarch passed on, his immediate descendants were already widely dispersed. One daughter, we know, was up north in Tennessee. A second lived to the west, in Birmingham, Alabama, and a third was settled to the south in Macon, Georgia. His eldest son, Novatus Jr., had stayed in West Point. His two half-brothers pushed on further to the west; one was located in Alabama, and another in Louisiana. When Novatus Lee Barker was born, automobiles did not exist and railroads were a novelty. When he died, men at war were on the verge of building jet engines, rockets, and atomic bombs. The technology of human dispersion has advanced considerably, though the patterns of our dispersal have not. If you have been thinking of Abraham's wandering as I have been walking with Novatus, then I have told his story well enough.

This patriarch's story ends very much like Abraham's, too. Novatus Lee Barker ended his days "gathered to his people"—in the west—facing onto what was probably a fairly underdeveloped field back then, one to which he was especially well-connected. He had already placed two children and two wives in the ground just there.

"Gathered to his people," says the Book . . . *his* people, and now—through the curious transactions borne of time, and the fond adoption of local space—*mine*, too. It's a pretty thought for day's end.

There is a very old American story—not so old by biblical standards perhaps, but old enough to matter—and it is the story of exile, an almost primal sense of dislocation. Most of the people who live in this land now are the descendants of ancestors who managed a *very* dangerous ocean crossing, willingly or no, to get here. The native inhabitants of this land were lost by and large, to themselves and to history, through the ironic self-fulfillment of the earliest colonists' prophetic self-understanding. If this were the *new* land of promise, and if they were the *new* Israel, then by wicked implication the prior inhabitants of the Americas were Canaanites, cursed by Noah and fit for destruction—all this, given the harsher Deuteronomic presuppositions of the day. (I have appended a few brief remarks to help explain this reference to Deuteronomy, which means "the second law" in Greek, at the close of this book.)

The old North American settler's story spans three generations. It needs all three to complete the cycle. First there are the grandparents, normally (but not always) two of them, who leave the old country for the so-called New World. They often do not learn the new language at all, resist assimilating, and cling to the dream of returning "home," even if they never do. Then comes the generation of the parents who are, in most ways that matter, caught *in between* two worlds, the old world and the new. Customarily bilingual, they are not tied to the Old World as their parents were; they tend to travel back and forth between the Old World and the new one, even if only for their vacations. Their cultural "identities" are ill-formed, at best—*if* clear borders are what you expect and need.[11] The Book rarely provides them. Neither does the New World. It is this third generation that is more thoroughly assimilated, children completely of this New World now, no longer feeling the same significant attachment to the place that had been home to their grandparents. They speak the New World's language, not the old one, and their tribal memories grow dimmer. Often enough, only their religion remains, and even that is different, if only due to the change in customs and climate and locale.

That story, as I have summarized it here, is *not* the story of persons of African descent in the New World, persons who did not travel with a biblical self-understanding in the beginning, and who in most cases did not come by choice. They lost their religions as well as their Old World languages. In the face of that cataclysmic cultural loss, the matter of their tribal memories is complex, indeed. And often irrecoverable. What is needed is a vast imagination, and careful attention. Coming to terms with how to tell the story of the West African diaspora, and how to graft it onto the larger narrative of American-ness, is one of the singular challenges facing most American cultures, north and south, at the dawn of the twenty-first century. Aware as I am of this deep dilemma, I can only wish for the moral imagination to find the appropriate genre, and the artistry, to tell this story better than I have done. In the interim, one can only be grateful for poetic voices like those of Toni Morrison, Ralph Ellison, Derek Walcott, C. L. R. James, and Maya Angelou, who help us all to see more—to see more clearly what has been lost, *and* what we might yet achieve.

With that all-important moral caveat, it is significant to notice that this age-old story of exile and resettlement is the story of the biblical patriarchs, too. Fully four hundred years later, in yet *another* Egyptian exile, Moses still refers to his God as "the God of Abraham, of Isaac, *and of*

---

11. An elegant criticism of this kind of reasoning, and this kind of need, is David Hollinger's *Postethnic America*.

Jacob."[12] Why all three? Why not just "the God of Abraham?" In short, because Canaan was no more Abraham's home than Egypt was. Canaan is *Jacob's* home, not his grandfather's. Abraham was forced to *leave* his home—first at Ur, and then again at Harran—forced into exile and resident aliency, in the very first moment that God assigned a special role to him.[13] It is one of the most moving things about his story, I think, one of the reasons for his singular and enduring appeal in several religious traditions. Philo's brilliant allegories are one especially, and Platonically, inspired way of expressing this movement. Abraham is forced into exile, forced to acknowledge an entirely new, and entirely foreign, world as his own. Yet he never really forgets where he came from, somewhere back among the greener pastures of Mesopotamia, the land "between the rivers."

This weird traveler's trajectory—from west to east, and back again—becomes all the more interesting when we learn later that Abraham actually served the traditional gods[14]—whether of Ur, or of Harran, or of Canaan, or of all three, we cannot definitively say. In the land of Canaan, after the covenant has been established and accepted, this probably means that he recognized and respected them, respected the native peoples' rights to their own religion, which is all natural enough for a vulnerable resident alien very far from his own home.[15] If Abraham was a monotheist, then he was a rather loose and free-wheeling one, far more tolerant of native religions and cultures than most latter-day monotheists have tended to be. This is one reason why theologians refer to him as a *heno*theist, a one-god-among-many-others man, rather than a strict *mono*theist. That would make him more of a one-god-is-all-I-can-allow-even-to-you man ... and this Abraham very clearly was not.

When Sarah died, Abraham's thoughts turned to his legacy, and thus to the arrangement of a marriage for his son. This arrangement required a journey; a journey Abraham was too old to make. Abraham wanted

12. Exod 2:24, 3:14–15.
13. Gen 12:1.
14. Josh 24:2.
15. The Israelites apparently did the same thing, in the course of their four-hundred-year enslavement in Egypt. See Josh 24:14.

to ensure that his son would marry a woman from the *old* country, by specifically sending his servant to the city of Nahor to arrange the match (this is very near to Harran, where Abraham's own father died and was buried). Rebecca (her Hebrew name is Rivka) is the result.[16]

The language surrounding Isaac's union with Rebecca is as curious and mysterious as his character. The boy is obviously deeply sensitive—and I don't think we are meant to forget the massive trauma he experienced at the hands of his father and his God when he was a boy. We meet him walking in his fields. It is late in the day, gliding gently toward sunset, and he is simply walking, presumably lost in thought, when Rebecca arrives.[17] *y-tz-'* is the Hebrew root that is used here in relation to Isaac; it can mean "strolling," and it can mean "pondering," and may even connote some combination of the two. I do it nearly every morning in my garden. That, in any case, is how Philo imagined him, in one of his more rhapsodic answers to a Genesis-question. In this case, the question concerns the association of "laughter" with such a traumatic story and such a sad child.

> Oh contemplation fitting to God and worthy intellection and vision, which was deserving of being commemorated in song, and most excellent vision, which the eye of the body cannot see! Therefore, O mind, with thy psychic eyes opened behold him who is within thee as an example of unsorrowing laughter, Isaac . . .[18]

That seems a bit of a stretch, turning Isaac into a symbol of *un*sorrowing, and it's clearly more than the Hebrew tells us. But Philo is an artful allegorist, schooled in the sacred arts of midrashic and Platonic philosophy. He's good at making up stories, or else simply finding what he wants in them. Philo engaged in spiritual allegorizing, intended to uncover the meaning of myth, rather than the morals of the (his)tories. (That's why the rabbis rarely read him, but some Greeks *loved* him). One thing is clear: Isaac is a sensitive soul, deeply grieved by the loss of his mother, and Rebecca is specifically described in the Book as a sort of surrogate, and as a comfort to him in his grief—much, perhaps, as Keturah was for his father, though less is made of this possibility in the texts we possess.

16. Gen 24:2–61.
17. Gen 24:63.
18. Philo *Questions and Answers on Genesis* 4.138.

All such matters are speculation, or midrash, or both. Tellingly enough, Isaac takes Rebecca into his *mother's* tent. He loves her, and makes a home with her, just there.[19] And that is how he is comforted, after the loss of his mother, Sarah.

In a very real sense, Isaac belongs nowhere. Second-generation immigrants rarely do. The biblical story idles, in fact, just so long as Isaac is in the foreground. His career is best described as the re-traversing of old ground, re-covering the wanderer's paths his father charted out before him. He re-digs the wells his father dug in the south, wells that Philistines have let fall into disuse or else have deliberately stopped up;[20] he re-visits altars and slaughter-sites dedicated to the awe-full God of his father;[21] he walks the length and breadth of this land that his descendants, too, will eventually populate and possess. He confirms his father's "title" to portions of the land of Canaan, and he does so without quite the same baggage of attachment to the other, older world in the east. But the larger story of life in the land of Canaan stalls under Isaac. He is a second-generation man; that is his special curse.

Isaac's sons seem to be freer to marry Canaanites, or any other women, if they so choose. His eldest son, Esau, does so; he marries two Hittite women named Judith and Basemath.[22] It is *Rebecca*—who *is* from the old country, we may recall—who determines that her younger son, Jacob, will *not* do this.[23] Jacob appears to receive a blessing for this, and so Esau takes a third wife, a woman named Mahalath, one of the daughters of Ishmael this time.[24] She is a slightly more "native" daughter, closer certainly to the family. But it is too late. Jacob's story has by now captured the attention of the mother, of the Book, and presumably of its audience. Jacob takes to wandering *'artzah b'ney-qedem*, "to the land of the Easterners,"[25] and he happens upon the city of Harran—the selfsame city where his great-grandfather is buried—and he eventually marries two sisters from this, his mother's hometown. They are Rachel and Leah;[26]

19. Gen 24:67.
20. Gen 26:18.
21. Gen 26:23–25.
22. Gen 26:34, though the next verse suggests that this was a bitter mistake.
23. Gen 27:46—28:5.
24. Gen 28:8–9.
25. Gen 29:1, literally he "lifts his feet toward the land of the sons of the east."
26. Gen 29:2–30.

Anita Diamant describes this tortuous extended family, its troubles and its triumphs, with rare poetic insight in *The Red Tent*, a book I've commended before. Diamant understands all too well that, while Jacob spent fourteen years there, the place was never really his home.

It is Jacob, then, this third-generation Chaldean-Canaanite, who is the first one fully and completely to embrace his new world. It is he who feels like a *foreigner*, ironically enough, in Harran. He refers to Canaan now as "*my* place" and "*my* land."[27] God refers to it as "the land of *your fathers*" as well.[28] And so it has finally become. Jacob is spectacularly successful in the land of Canaan, maybe even more than his grandfather was. It belongs to him, and he to it. Not the most compelling of biblical characters, morally or otherwise, Jacob nevertheless has many children,[29] and each of his sons will be the eponymous founder of an "Israelite" tribe. Sure, there are other forks in the road they might have marked, or taken, but when it comes time for his descendants to name themselves as an independent nation—as a *people*—they will turn to Jacob for a name,[30] not to his father or his grandfather. These people think of themselves as Israelites—not Abrahamites or Isaacites, as we might have expected. I think that there are subtle reasons for that: Only with Jacob is the grand transition, which began with Abraham's obedient wandering westward, complete. While famine and family troubles eventually force him into a southern exile in Egypt as well, Jacob extracts a formal oath from his favored younger son, Joseph, that his body will be duly returned to Canaan for burial.[31] *That* place, and *only* that place, is home now.

In fact, almost *all* of these first three generations will be buried together, poignantly enough, in that eloquent little cave at Makhpela, facing east on Mamre—a plot of ground that this family arguably knew better than any other place in the world. Abraham laid out his wife, Sarah, there.[32] Isaac and Ishmael laid out Abraham there as well.[33] Isaac installed

---

27. Gen 30:25.

28. Gen 31:3.

29. Gen 35:22–26.

30. Or rather to "Israel," the name God gave him, which is nearly the same thing, but not quite. See Gen 32:28.

31. Gen 47:29–30.

32. Gen 23:19.

33. Gen 25:9–10.

Rebecca in this cave,[34] and Jacob laid out Isaac in turn, with Esau's help.[35] Jacob was unable to place his beloved Rachel there, for she died unexpectedly in childbirth, very far from their home.[36] But he did bury his other wife—Leah, her sister—in this growing family mausoleum.[37] And all of his sons returned from Egypt just long enough to install Jacob's mummy in the tomb as well.[38]

The story of Genesis, from Adam to Abraham, begins and ends in a garden. It is the garden that links together these two essential biblical tropes: attachment to place, on the one hand; the image of wandering, uprooting and exile, on the other. There is a tension between these ideals, between the need for roots and an inexhaustible human restlessness. God gardened in the east. But we lost our grip on this originary garden, were exiled from it, perhaps necessarily, and were destined in any case to till other ground, on our own. Abraham—who is just another exile, at the beginning of this story—tilled it first in a pretty little copse of oak trees, near a field called Mamre and a complicated cave at Makhpela. So the cycle of Genesis begins and ends in a garden.

All three of the biblical patriarchs reside together in their new world, in the very first plot that the very first of them had purchased, claimed, and cultivated, making it his very own. Earlier, I wondered if Abraham cultivated a garden there in that well-loved field at Mamre. This is the main reason I wonder. God, after all, gardened in the east. But this same God determined that we should till the soil elsewhere, further to the west. It's a pretty thought for evening, as we do what we do each day, chasing after the sun, then the moon, by turns.

34. Gen 49:31.
35. Gen 35:27–29.
36. Gen 35:16–20.
37. Gen 49:31.
38. Gen 50:7–14.

chapter eleven
WAKING

Half the fun of a garden, I believe, is to try out odd plants from all over the world, and if we deliberately banish experiments we risk losing a lot of pleasure. . . . Furthermore, I have come to realize that, as we enter the third millennium, gardening is turning a sharp corner. The old elitist gardens of the aristocracy—reserved for the privileged few—have shown themselves to be out of date. . . . We are beginning to realize that the main task for humanity today is not to design charming gardens but to solve ecological crisis; to come to grips with the problem of overpopulation, industrial pollution and destruction of the natural eco-systems upon which our lives depend. We realize too that our unnatural lifestyles—revolving around fast cars, obsessive over-consumption and passive entertainment—are quite literally killing us. . . .

But the world is not like this for the experienced gardener. Time is our friend; everything will be prettier and greener tomorrow; every seed we plant is a thrilling promise and every tree will grow nobler and stronger with each passing year. We look forward to the next year and the next five years in our gardens with happy anticipation, not dread. This waiting and watching is a hopeful and not a fearful thing and we become, while watching our seedlings grow, philosophers.

This relaxed attitude has also brought another dividend—my garden no longer lays claim to my exclusive attention. There is another world out there and if I want to find out how the daturas bloom in Amalfi and how they prune lemon trees in Sicily I can go to see for myself. And when someone suggests a trip to Puglia or, better yet, to Karnataka and Kerala, I can be packed up and ready in a matter of days with lots of empty envelopes waiting for seeds.

A garden should not be an anchor, it should be a spinnaker ready to catch the best winds that blow, and if the wind is right it can blow you to places of breathtaking beauty.[1]

. . .

I awoke this morning with a strange-seeming question weighing on my mind. It's been hard for me to get a firm handle on it, even after a long yesterday of quiet meditation on the Book. And the longer I've been fussing over it this morning, the more worried I've become—not a good feeling, for a gardener who's supposed to be in the business of cultivating delight. To put it as simply as I can, the thing is this: *I can't tell whether Abraham had any friends.* I am thinking about the people who *really* loved him, which means, at a minimum, that they'd shared a considerable stretch of road with him, and presumably learned him well enough to appreciate him for who he was. My question assumes that these same people could actually have *known* Abraham, which—as Kierkegaard concluded in dismay, if not quite the sudden borderline disgust that I am feeling—is nearly impossible. If no one really knew him, then I'm hard-pressed to imagine how he could have had either friends or lovers. I think of his negotiations for Sarah's burial plot again in this light, and I'm far more disturbed by the story now: whoever he's negotiating with, they are not friends, anything but that. Fear and awe, while they can mysteriously come, and very rarely even stay, hand in hand with love, need to be kept distinct from that sacred emotion. Blurring these lines too much kills them both. Love finds a way past awe to intimacy. "It is bigamy to love and dream."[2]

The sons of Het certainly feared Abraham and stood in awe of him, but I see no evidence that they loved him. Quite to the contrary. And as for Sarah . . . well, she dies, as so many biblical women do, with the words

---

1. Marble, *Notes From an Italian Garden*, 338–43.
2. Elytis, *Maria Nephele*, "Nefelegeretes."

stifled in her throat. Silent, aggrieved. Did Abraham love *her*? Or did he love the *land*? What was he really negotiating with the sons of Het? A burial plot? Or a foothold—first for his family, and then for a nation?

What Abraham had was *family*, not friends, an almost astonishing superabundance of family.[3] Ishmael came first, of course, an eldest son whose descendants are now claimed as Ishmael-ite Arabs, the very camel nomads and Bedouin to whom God would later send a prophet, and through whom God would speak in words the Qur'an is said to preserve. They are mostly Muslims now, "those who submit." And what they say about Abraham is interesting. The most common Qur'anic epithet for Abraham is *khali-Allah*, "the friend of God." But he's only imagined as a friend *of God*, a Book-ish attitude that is confirmed in those most *in*human of all historical chronicles, the later biblical histories.[4] The Qur'an also properly reminds us that Abraham was neither Jewish nor Christian, since neither the Law nor the Gospel had been revealed yet.[5] Abraham had *no* religious community; in the beginning, his was an army (and a family) of One. He later condemned even his own father for idolatry.[6] And while "true believers, both men and women, are friends to one another,"[7] Abraham's faith was his alone—and thus, entirely friendless in the beginning. No community. No village. No friends. Just a rich, and often violent, legacy.

Abraham sired Isaac next, through whom the Book will trace the subsequent line of a privileged grandson, Jacob. His descendants, traced further through twelve sons who gave their names to twelve tribes and were originally called Israel-ites, are remembered today as Judah-ites, or "Jews." The relationship between these two forks in the family road—Isaac's and Ishmael's—have been fraught, as family relations so often are. *Family are not friends*; it seems especially important to keep this in mind,

---

3. It seems worth noting that this emphasis on family relations to the virtual exclusion of others seems more of a peasant mentality, a country mentality if you will, than it is a citied one. The biblical patriarchs all lived in the wilderness and eyed big cities with deep suspicion. By contrast, the Greeks who philosophized about friendship did so in cities (*poleis*) where such friendship was understood as the very foundation of their "politics."

4. 2 Chr 20:7.

5. Qur'an 3:65-67.

6. Qur'an 26:70-80.

7. Qur'an 9:71.

when confronting the message in the Book. This the Greeks knew well; Greek tragedy is many things, but it is *not* romantic in its views of the nuclear family.

Anything but that—Greek tragedy sees the family as a locus of singular violence, and often of human horror. Friends are those who help us carry that burden. And to begin again.

Abraham had a bevy of other children—six sons are named, and their descendants carefully catalogued in the Book[8]—all with a native Canaanite woman named Keturah. Their family identity is more complicated, and they became more dispersed—to the east, naturally. Perhaps some Christians, who claim a subtler filial relation to Abraham, almost as if they are *adoptive* children,[9] can identify with this more mysterious eastern branch of the family. Abraham seems to have sent these later children packing well before his own death, returning them to the eastland, closer to his own home in Mesopotamia, among the Chaldeans. That brought them back to *his* home, closer to modern-day Iraq, where we in the U.S. are waging yet one more war, killing and dying in a haze of frustration, and a land overly dense with scriptural and religious histories. Abraham's legacy, it sometimes seems, is *everywhere*. And "middle eastern" (yes, *eastern*) politics can seem like a not-so-subtle family-affair, one in which friendship scarcely appears as an imagined possibility on the horizon of our failing hopes.

God promised Abraham a host of descendants too numerous to name or count; it will be as futile to try to do that as it would be to count soft grains of sand on a Mediterranean shoreline, or twinkling stars in a desert sky. That sacred art of counting was always more of a Greek preoccupation, and a Greek art, than ever it was a Hebraic one. This little gardener's book began with that contrast and I am even more mindful of its importance now, at the end. Socrates suggested that meditative and essentially spiritual practices such as counting carefully, and composing poetry, and loving well—all in the hungry pursuit of wonder, and of more musing sorts of knowledge—defined the very "method" to which he'd married himself, and defined a path to which he remained faithful all of his life. Plato believed that Socrates had died in its name. As I suggested at the beginning, this Socratic kind of counting involves the subtle art of

---

8. Gen 25:1–4.
9. Rom 4:1–25.

moving from one, to the many, to the limitless—from Abraham, to his children, to the nearly countless Jews, Christians, and Muslims peopling the planet today. It takes a lot of time to think that staging through, time to pause at each step along the thinker's way, marking out each of the station-stops on a vast pilgrimage toward sacred numbers. It demands an august and profound attention; it also requires a vast philosophical patience. It demands the skills of reverie and the special wisdom of a gardener, as I have been learning over many slow years spent working here in mine.

Abraham's descendants, his extended and extensive family, are described as virtually limitless; no one will be able to count them all, and some will die trying. There are close to three billion of them, now—that's a lot of descendants to count. And it's one reason why Abraham is remembered as the "father" of *many* peoples—a father of tribes, or ethnicities, or, in our more modern parlance, of "nations" and their "religions." It's one reason why later, *non*-Jewish Godward-types—whether Christian, Muslim, or Neoplatonic—so often came wandering back to his character, desiring not to understand him, which is impossible, but rather to establish some sort of relationship to him, a *familial* one if at all possible. Abraham didn't seem to know any other kind. I am emphasizing that point because I'm stuck just there: the Book always conceived this story as a *family* romance, and a *family* affair. No one in the Book, as nearly as I can tell, ever claimed to be Abraham's *friend*. My problem is that I am not from his family, and I am no longer certain that I want to be his friend.

When Abraham rounded out his life after 175 years of nearly constant wandering, his body came to rest in that storied plot I've remarked upon before: "the cave of Makhpela, in the field of Efron son of Tzohar the Hittite, that faces Mamre, the field that Abraham had acquired from the sons of Het."[10] That's a pretty rich description for a mere burial plot; it seems yet again almost as if *the land* matters as much as the people buried in it do. That is a daring and unusual way to view things, but not a very attractive or human one.

Abraham's life was very long: over sixty thousand days; one and a half million hours; ninety million minutes; well over five and one-half *billion* (that's with a *B*) seconds. The philosopher in me gasps, then shudders with a careful counter's disbelief. But the poet in me hesitates, then

---

10. Gen 25:9–10.

stalls, realizing that his heart, for all that it had been through and all those he had lost or buried, beat at least that many times, strong to the end. It's no small feat to live that long, simply to keep it going. Going with God. More striking by Greek standards is the manner of his passing away. It is remarkable that his two eldest sons—Isaac *and* Ishmael, the rival half-brothers so long estranged—took his body in hand together, and together they laid him out in the cave, beside his first wife. This is a remarkable symbol of the power of Abraham's unseverable family connections. Ishmael, be sure to recall, had been cast out with his mother, yea those long years ago. It is sure testimony to the power of *his* person that Ishmael traveled all the way from the desert midlands to help his half-brother lay the old man's body to rest.[11] It is still surer testimony to the largeness of spirit of the son that he honors his filial duties in this way, making a long trip surely no one would have required him to make. The Book emphasizes Ishmael's goodness, in the end. He, too, has a wealth of descendants, twelve sons in all, sons who became the eponymous founders of twelve Ishmaelite tribes.[12] So Ishmael accomplishes in a single generation what his half-brother Isaac could not. Isaac's son, Jacob, in the *next* generation, will finally accomplish a feat to rival what Ishmael did on his own: he starts down the long road to countlessness. "Ishmaelites and Israelites," twelve tribes apiece. The Book emphasizes that parallelism, before it zooms in to trace Isaac's and Jacob's story-line in greater detail. They are just one impossibly large, impossibly dispersed family now.

I am emphasizing what the Book does not, because I'm haunted by it. True, Abraham was "gathered to his people" in the old oak grove at Mamre, but his "people" are strictly kin.[13] The term is obscure in Hebrew (*el-'ammân*), and it's an ambiguous phrase in the Septuagint's Greek as well (*ton laon autou*), but the context makes it clear enough . . . by telling us who's absent. There is no mention of a single *friend* at Abraham's funeral, not even the sons of Het, his nearest neighbors, the ones who sold this gravesite to him, once upon a time. Abraham is all about his family, with no room left for friends. And he dies very nearly alone—with two sons and an unmentioned Canaanite wife—in the telling absence of everyone else.

---

11. Gen 25:18.
12. Gen 25:14–16.
13. Gen 25:8.

It was the *non*-Abrahamic Greeks who would develop a more probing philosophy of friendship and would meditate fruitfully on its intimate connection to another kind of passionate desire. This one they called *erôs*. The Greeks seem as obsessed with the ideas of friendship, and of love, as the Book[14] seems silent about them. The Greeks were to develop a dramatic and almost ecstatic philosophy of friendship—a picture of human life embedded in a web of passionate, often lifelong, human attachments—which they communicated with poetic inspiration, great style, and memorable rhetorical sweep. I am thinking of certain gorgeous Platonic dialogues, like the *Lysis*, *Symposium*, and *Phaedrus*, which Philo tried to weave into his own whimsical meditations on Genesis. I am also recalling that two out of ten books in Aristotle's *Nicomachean Ethics* were dedicated to the same constellation of ideas, suggesting that friendship, not family, lay at the very center of the moral life as most Greeks understood it.[15] I am thinking finally of the important generic twins: *lyric-erotic* poetry on the one hand, and *tragic* poetry on the other, genres that the invention of the vowel made possible—that almost alchemical process of linking disparate things together, and making them stay. That's how Anne Carson invites us to imagine these developments in the Greek language *and* in the rich adventure of Greek thinking. I've become convinced with time in my garden that she's right. The difference between the Greek and Hebrew ways of writing makes other differences possible, maybe even necessary.

I have raised this concern before, and I raise it again here now at the end. What Joan Marble says about gardens and gardeners goes for books and their readers, too. The Book is not supposed to be a deadening anchor; it's supposed to be a spinnaker that sets you sailing on a life of wonder, of careful counting, of poetic whimsy, and divine inspiration. In order to read the Book well, you will need other books too. In order to inhabit a family well, or a land, you will need friends. We North Americans are quick to congratulate ourselves on our commitments to pluralism, diversity, and multiculturalism. We think of our politics as friendly (external appearances notwithstanding), and name those who oppose these

---

14. With the howling exceptions of the prophecies of Hosea, of the friendship between David and Jonathan, and of several lovely verses in King Solomon's Song of Songs.

15. I am indebted to my good friend, Peter Murphy, who invited me to contribute to his guest-edited volume of the South Atlantic Quarterly, "Friendship," in 1998. This got me started on a line of enquiry which culminates in these pages.

ideals "fundamentalists." And so many of them are. The trouble is, you don't get anywhere by calling a name-caller names. You can't fight Islamic fundamentalism with Christian or Jewish or secular versions of the same thing. If you are serious about Judaism and its history, then you should read the New Testament. If you are serious about Christianity and its history, then you should read the Qur'an. And if you are serious about any of this, serious about being a descendant of Abraham—about being a member of what the Qur'an characterizes as a singular and far-flung community of friends, "the people of the Book"[16]—then you should read other books, too. *Greek* books, I think. There is an especially long, proud history, as well as a set of inspiring historical examples never more precious and relevant than now, of Jews and Christians and Muslims coming together to discuss the books they have in common. While they all had Abraham in common, speaking mythologically, most of the *books* they had in common were Greek books. They couldn't really debate about "scripture," because they didn't have the same ones. But they could argue about Plato and Aristotle . . . and did so. If there is ever to be a way out of the mess that the children of Abraham have created for themselves and for the rest of us, then it will require some careful Greek counting, and some careful Greek thinking. Because the dramatic promise symbolized by the invention of Greek vowels is the perennial promise of the possibility of bringing harsh and discordant things together into a harmony.

There is another Greek obsession that is nearly as prominent in their literature as their personal interests in friendship and the romantic life are. They called it "politics," the art and craft of learning to live in a community, the signature form of *Greek* political community, the *polis*. This concern seems absent from the Book, somehow—at least as long as those not-so-bookish biblical patriarchs preferred life in a desert to cities. Surrounded as he is by a multitude of extended family relations, and a sea of more casual acquaintances, Abraham still seems like a remarkably isolated figure to me. He's a loner, utterly apolitical, and we usually meet him in the Book when he is alone. His relationship with his God is simply the most mysterious and ineffable of his many strange relations. A rather truncated form of politics grows out of a patriarchal wilderness vision like this one. Those who saw themselves in *that* story, when first they achieved a quasi-empire of their own, could imagine no further

---

16. This is stated in its most elaborate and challenging form at Qur'an 5:59–82.

aspiration than becoming "like the other nations."[17] I know the Book is ambivalent about that; still, that *is* what the people said they wanted, the entire substance of their political dreams. Greek "politics," by contrast, became an extended meditation on, and an aspiration toward, an entirely *new* political way-of-being. It wasn't imperial; that came later, with Alexander the Great. Then Rome. And while Alexander and Augustus achieved great and wondrous things, they also sounded the death-knell of the independent Greek city-state, and her literature, and her politics.

Like Abraham—and I know I'm stretching here, but I can think of no other way to wrap this up—empires rarely have friends. They are as aloof, as alone, and often as incomprehensible as the alleged hero of the Akedah. Empires have alliances, relations of mutual convenience, coercive deals rooted more in fear than fellow-feeling. It's devilishly hard to get to know an empire, especially if you happen to be one of its colonies, and it's harder still to feel any loving attachment to one. As I said in the introduction to this gardener's tale, empires often don't even know themselves, don't recognize until fairly late in the game who and what they have allowed themselves to become. Imperial self-knowledge comes late, if and when it comes at all. If imperial politics is to have any real civility or decency or intelligence, then it's incumbent upon empires to know themselves, to admit what they have become—in the eyes of others, and in their own eyes. We desperately need such a perspective in this country now—unblinking, honest, thoughtful, and more careful. We need to grow up, and we need an adult form of politics we deserve but do not often demand. To do any of our current work well, we *will* need friends, and need to listen better to them when they are trying to tell us who and what we have become, by pointing out to us the things we tend to overlook, or wish to ignore. They are the USA's closest friends, not her enemies, who have been trying to show us that we have, in fact, taken up the mantle of an empire. We can seem as isolated and inscrutable as Abraham. And our true friends do not want our paternalism, nor our brand of protection. As the probing Roman historian, Tacitus, put the criticism of his own age's imperialisms in jarring terms: "they create a desert, and call it peace."[18] Peace is not a place where there is no one left to count. Peace exists rather only among friends.

17. 1 Sam 8:5.
18. Tacitus *Agricola* §30.

Our current troubles began in a desert of sorts, commercially and innocently enough, after the Great Depression and a Second World War; it's all far more deliberate now, largely because our power today is more military than mercantile. Whereas our Texas-rich oil interests in the Middle East date back to the 1950s, the real change in the region and its posture came when we established several air bases in Saudi Arabia in 1990—nominally to launch a defensive assault against an Iraqi regime we had helped arm in the previous decade, against the threat we then perceived in the Ayatollah Khomeini's Iran, itself supported and armed by the Soviets. The trouble is, those bases stayed long after the first Gulf War ended in 1991; we needed them to patrol the southern "No-Fly Zone" we enforced with British assistance until the second Gulf War began.

In the eyes of a Bedouin-inspired primitivist like Osama bin Laden (whose career began fighting those same Soviets in the mountains of Afghanistan, with U.S. assistance, though we seem to prefer political amnesia where men such as Saddam Hussein and Osama bin Laden are concerned), that's when it all came apart. Bin Laden had it out for the Empire that owned these bases, *and* for the Saudi regime that permitted them to be built on holy land. His attitudes, inspired by the haunting desert image of Abraham, and a later generation of hardened Ishmaelite malcontents, are hardly his alone.[19] We simply cannot responsibly ignore the depth and the intensity of anti-American sentiments, worldwide. If we were to be shown a world map, one that indicated, country by country, how many service-men and -women we have stationed there, I believe the collective gasp in the U.S. electorate would be heard worldwide. Such are the belated realizations to which empires are probably always latecomers. This second war is decidedly *not* about oil; it is about military bases, and an elusive desire for security. I have no doubt that this administration is committed to Iraq's nominal political independence, but our bases in Saudi Arabia have all been moved to southern Iraq, and they will not leave. If there is a link between the tragic events of September 11, 2001, and this second Gulf War in Iraq, then it is to be found here, and *only* here. That the Bush administration fails to say this clearly is but one on a long list of its political missteps, rapidly becoming, like the casualties, too numerous to count.

19. This becomes very clear in Bruce Lawrence's edited volume of Osama bin Laden's speeches, entitled *Messages to the World*.

As I've struggled with these conflicting political self-images over the past several years, I have been unable to shake the unsettling feeling that Abraham, along with Socrates, has something to contribute to our understanding of what's been happening in this country and abroad over the unbearably long last three-and-seventy months. It might have something to do with injecting a more sober Socratic friendship, some simple compassion and decency, into our politics, however edgy with imperialism and raw power it may also be. It's clearly got a lot to do with Abraham—with his descendants, and their quarrels, and their inscrutable God.

But Hebrew had no vowels. And Abraham had no friends. Nor lovers, not in the Greek (or modern) sense of that term. That seems as important to reflect upon[20] as it is to ask a question that follows almost inescapably once we see it: In the absence of all that, these deep and abiding threads of human connection, what *did* Abraham have? One thing upon which all three of the scriptural monotheisms agree is the fact that Abraham had *faith*, a flamboyant and almost surreal obedience in the face of his perception of divine commands. Abraham hears, and he obeys. He always obeys. He's a lot like Cadmus that way. Minus the vowels. And Harmony.[21]

In dramatic contrast to Abraham, and a bit more like Socrates and the rest of us, I've been richly blessed with extraordinary friends, an extensive tribe of gifted and remarkable people, people who really do know me, I think, and who love without reservation or condition. This book is

20. As I tried to do, with admittedly limited success, in *Symposia: Plato, the Erotic and Moral Value*.

21. Jeffrey Stout reminds me that this is not uniformly the case. In fact, there are two events that I failed to discuss when I looked at the strange story of Sodom in the chapter called "Fire." One of them concerns the mysterious blessing Abram receives from Melchizedek (Gen 14:17–21); this story has been expanded in one of the oddest of all New Testament midrashim, in the Letter to the Hebrews, chapter 7. I must confess that I've never known what to make of this story, precisely because the two men have no prior relationship and are completely unknown to each other. The second story demonstrates Abram's willingness to quarrel with, and to bargain with, his God. Abram asks if God will relent from the destruction of the city of Sodom if as few as ten just persons are found to reside there, and God consents to this (Gen 18:22–33). That Abram is willing to speak in this fashion on behalf, once again, of persons whom he does not know, but not to do so on behalf of his own son, is one of the many distressing aspects of his character as it is presented in the Book. At times, it can appear as if the most privileged position of all is that of the stranger (who may be, and often is, God), he who is neither family nor friend. It is very hard to imagine what kind of politics emerges from such a narrow view.

dedicated to them, because neither it nor my garden could possibly have come into being without them. And while I was alone all day yesterday, musing and gardening, reading and thinking, tonight they are coming over for an autumnal harvest feast, and I'll devote the balance of this day to gathering, then cooking and baking, then feasting in their fond company. These days remind me of what the garden is ultimately for: sacred forms of connection. To the soil. To the creation. To those we love. Yesterday's musings, which admittedly gave birth to a little book, can't compare to tonight's largesse. I just can't make out if Abraham ever came to such an understanding. He couldn't write, he couldn't read, and I'm uncertain whether he ever gardened.

Like Novatus Lee Barker, I've sown in southern soil for a pretty long time. How to marry my own Hellenic inclinations to these Hebrew musings has been one of my main preoccupations in this book. Marrying images from biblical lives and biblical stories to my own sense of place has been another. A lot hinges on Abraham, I've come to see—how you read his stories, how you understand his movements and his motives, the details you take the time to notice. If he didn't have friends or lovers, then what *did* he have in their place? "Faith" no longer seems a sufficient answer to that question, not to me, not by a long shot.

Today we continue to fight and die in ancient Mesopotamia, close to where Abraham was born. While tragically misguided, the toppling of a regime in Iraq has been linked by our leaders to two toppled towers here at home. The collective trauma of those shattering events in New York City, and Washington DC, and a lonely Pennsylvanian cornfield was overwhelming, and sometimes seems nearly as raw today as it was more than five years ago. We still have not yet figured out how to commemorate it, nor to tell it properly. That was very clear when the nation tried to ritualize these events on a somber September anniversary one year later, tried to find the words to express it, and discovered that no words really came—just lists of victims, dead names, impossible to count. In the absence of *fresh* words suited to the day, they turned to *old* words instead, to the words of a very different Abraham, a figure just as august in North American folklore, and probably just as lonely, yet his words didn't really fit the moment either. They didn't apply to this, a vastly different kind of pain.

Perhaps if we had turned to Lincoln's Second Inaugural Address, instead of his more famous Gettysburg speech, we might have done a little better, gotten a little further down the road to a *different* place, a *new* place, emotionally and politically and spiritually. The Gettysburg Address was delivered in November of 1863; it is all about war and carnage. The Second Inaugural was delivered in March of 1865; it envisions a new peace, and coming back to life. Sometimes, a single year can make that much difference in the moral imagination. By then, the President had committed tremendous emotional and intellectual energy, and the very highest moral seriousness, to thinking about what the peace *after* the war could reasonably hope to resemble. Our failure to apply that same thinking in Iraq and Palestine is but a piece of a larger failure—the failure of moral imagination.

Lincoln had concluded his *first* inaugural address, just before the outbreak of the war, with a nod to "the better angels of our nature." He had desperately hoped to avoid this. Now, after four years of unimaginable slaughter, here is the place of peace he aimed the nation at, a place where simplistic and one-sided accusations of "good" and "evil" no longer had a place at all. It was a time for more careful moral accounting, a time for counting the real cost of war. Between friends.

> Neither [side] expected for the war the magnitude or the duration which it had already attained. . . . Both read the same Bible, and pray to the same God; and each invokes his aid against the other. It may seem strange that any men should dare to ask a just God's assistance in wringing their bread from the sweat of other men's faces; but let us judge not, that we be not judged. The prayers of both could not be answered—that of neither has been answered fully. . . .
>
> With malice toward none; with charity toward all; with firmness in the right, as God gives us to see the right, let us strive to finish the work we are in; to bind up the nation's wounds; to care for him who shall have borne the battle, and for his widow, and his orphan—to do all which may achieve and cherish a just and lasting peace among ourselves, and with all nations.[22]

Today, our politics seem mired in terror,[23] justifiably so at times, but fear and anger are clearly poor places and rude sentiments from which to render grand historical verdicts or to hatch grand imperial stratagems.

22. Stern, *Life and Writings of Abraham Lincoln*, 841–42.
23. Brilliantly analyzed in rhetorical terms by Winkler, *In theName of Terror*.

As Kierkegaard described the first Abraham (and be sure to recall that the second of them, Abraham Lincoln, was already a young man when the Dane wrote these lines): "you needed 100 years to get the son of your old age against all expectancy, . . . you had to draw the knife before you kept [him]; . . . in 130 years you got no further than faith."[24] I don't know what that means exactly, because I don't know that Abraham. And there we are. Stuck in the not-knowing. Even if you *want* to have faith.

What can such an invocation of "faith" mean, in the end? I'm afraid that, too often, it simply means to remind us that Abraham obeyed. When God demanded his son, he offered him up. I can't begin to know what to think about that. So I keep trying to ignore it, and it keeps coming back—like a rising, like a scar.

When God told Abraham to leave home, he left. That is perhaps the silent key to his whole character. He accepted the face of the unknown we often meet in others who seem strange to us. He faced down his own fear. He learned how *not* to be at home. And he trusted that, with time, we can be at home anywhere. What I'd like to add to what we know about this biblical Abraham—and it is the inescapably limiting feature of his character, for me—is some greater sensitivity to the central importance of friendship and of love. Abraham may have been at home on the land, but he was not among friends. These thoughts keep bringing me back to the garden, that garden in the east. In the ancient time, *before* Abraham. How to turn the foreign into a friend is the sacred task before us today. It is a Greek problem, I think. And requires a gardener's patience, I know.

One of the many gardeners I've met in these pages, one who is also an especially graceful writer and an especially prodigious ponderer, is Diane Ackerman. She's a counter, too, in the best Socratic style. Here is how she imagines the springtime, philosophically speaking. With a question.

> Is it spring yet? Spring travels north at about thirteen miles a day, which is 47.6 feet per minute, or about 1.23 inches per second. That sounds rather fast, and viewable.[25]

Sounds like it is, but it isn't, of course. Spring doesn't march across the garden like an army on the move, or even a surreptitious shadow in reverse. It comes in stops and starts. And, like seeds breaking ground—an

---

24. Kierkegaard, *Fear and Trembling*, 23.
25. Ackerman, *Cultivating Delight*, 242.

image much preferred by Jesus in many of his parables[26]—one day, it is all just magically *there*.

It is autumn now, not springtime. The time these two seasons take to travel is the same, but their mood is entirely different. I can feel summer fleeing, not arriving. What is coming is the winter, with all of its death and hunger and quiet dread. It is a time for armies to decamp, to come home. It is a time for the land to lie fallow, for the gardener to indulge in long afternoon naps before the fire, and, in its most dramatic form, for hibernation. The long sleep is coming, an inch and a second at a time. Staying awake in such a time is no small thing.

What the Book suggests is shattering in its clarity, whether we like it or no. God asks us to change places. God dares us to change. We perceive these changes as trauma. We resist them. And in the often unforgiving logic of genesis, we are reminded that this is our problem, not God's.

It took the Greeks, along with my garden, to help me sense some new lessons in all of this. It is Autumn again, and I am tired. There is a lovely word of ancient Greek pedigree: *exupnos*. Literally, it means "out [*ex*] of sleep [*hypnos*]," and thus by poetic implication, it means "waking up." In *modern* Greek, it's become their word for "wisdom," too, the sort of thing that enabled my philosopher-friend to count so much better than I.

It is long past time for children of Abraham—*all* of them, but most especially the ones who refuse to look past the boundaries of their Book or the borders of their Land—to awaken from a very long sleep. So that we can count something more than bodies, and plant something other than our dead.

---

26. Proverbially at Mark 4:1–9, but in many other places as well.

Appendix

First Law, Second Law, Divine Law

William Slothrop was a peculiar bird. He took off from Boston, heading west in true Imperial style, in 1634 or -5, sick and tired of the Winthrop machine, convinced he could preach as well as anybody in the hierarchy even if he hadn't been officially ordained. The ramparts of the Berkshires stopped everybody else at the time, but not William. He just started climbing. He was one of the very first Europeans in. After they settled in Berkshire, he and his son John got a pig operation going—used to drive the hogs right back down the great escarpment, back over the long pike to Boston, drive them just like sheep or cows. By the time they got to market those hogs were so skinny it was hardly worth it, but William wasn't really in it so much for the money as just for the trip itself. He enjoyed the road, the mobility, the chance encounters of the day—Indians, trappers, wenches, hill people—most of all just being with those pigs. They were good company. Despite the folklore and the injunctions in his own Bible, William came to love their nobility and personal freedom, their gift for finding comfort in the mud on a hot day—pigs out on the road, in company together, were everything Boston wasn't, and you can imagine what the end of the journey, the weighing, slaughter and dreary pigless return back up into the hills must've been like for William. Of course he took it as a parable—knew that the squealing bloody horror at the end of the pike was in exact balance to their happy sounds, their untroubled pink eyelashes and kind eyes, their smiles, their grace in cross-country movement. It was a little early for Isaac Newton, but feelings about action and reaction were in the air. . . .

He wrote a long tract about it presently, called *On Preterition*. It had to be published in England, and is among the first books to've been not only banned but also ceremoniously burned in Boston. Nobody wanted to hear about all the Preterite, the many God passes over when he chooses a few for salvation. William argued holiness for these "second Sheep," without whom there'd be no elect. You can bet the Elect in Boston were pissed off about that. And it got worse. William felt that what Jesus was for the elect, Judas Iscariot was for the Preterite, everything in the Creation has its equal and opposite counterpart. How can Jesus be an exception? . . .

How William avoided being burned for heresy, nobody knows. He must've had connections. They did finally 86 him out of Massachusetts Bay Colony—he thought about Rhode Island for a while but decided he wasn't that keen on antinomians either. So finally he sailed back to Old England, not in disgrace so much as despondency, and that's where he died, among memories of the blue hills, green maizefields, get-togethers over hemp and tobacco with the Indians, young women in upper rooms with their aprons lifted, pretty faces, hair spilling on the wood floors while underneath in the stables horses kicked and drunks hollered, the starts in the very early mornings when the backs of his herd glowed like pearl, the long, stony and surprising road to Boston, the rain on the Connecticut River. . . .

Could he have been the fork in the road America never took, the singular pinpoint she jumped the wrong way from? Suppose the Slothropite heresy had had time to consolidate and prosper? Might there have been fewer crimes in the name of Jesus, and more mercy in the name of Judas Iscariot? It seems to Tyrone Slothrop that there might be a route back—maybe that anarchist he met in Zurich was right, maybe for a little while all the fences are down, one road as good as another, the whole space of the Zone cleared, depolarized. . . . Such are the vistas of thought that open up in Slothrop's head as he tags along. . . . Is he drifting, or being led?[1]

1. Pynchon, *Gravity's Rainbow*, 647–48.

...

The first twenty-five chapters of the Hebrew Bible are not at all "Deuteronomic"—with its see-sawing divine justice and almost theatrical cruelty, a world that veers wildly back and forth between obedience and blessing, then disobedience and savage punishment. For this very reason, these early chapters of Genesis may well tell a story better suited to the moral sensibilities of the early twenty-first century, an age duly and increasingly suspicious of overly simple moral judgments, though God knows we still long for them. One need not be a Nietzschean to be suspicious of the casual ease with which some would couch *every* battle as a war "between good and evil." This holds even for the current U.S. President. When "they" call us evil, we reject them as fanatics. When we call "them" evil, we see ourselves as righteous defenders of our nation and of our God. Nothing is as simple as that, and I've become convinced in the last several years that I would not want to live in a world as simple as that. The ethics you encounter in a garden are subtle, nuanced, and complex. In any case, the Book paints a very clear picture of where that sort of reasoning leads: to massive exterminations, whether in the land of Canaan or in the New World. As I have been reading and re-reading the Book, I have been intrigued, and vaguely comforted, to see that It does *not* say such things are simple. After the twinned hammer-blows of Fall and Flood, even God has become wary of the language of good and evil.

It seems as if we actually see three separate theological attitudes to the existence of evil and suffering in the world described by the Book. By implication, we also get three separate attitudes to divine justice and divine justification, what theologians call "theodicy," and what that preeminently modern philosopher, Hegel, would eventually claim was actually the real work of the history of the world. This wide range of perspectives is already evident in the Torah, the first five books of the Hebrew Bible alleged to have been penned by Moses himself (even though they conclude with a description of his own death and mysterious burial[2]).

At the first, then, we meet a *Dualist* position, one that posits *two* creative forces at work in the world, and pits the forces of disruption (symbolized by the waters of Chaos, by the serpent, and perhaps even by humanity itself) against the foundational goodness of God. Everything we know as evil is born of the conflict between these two forces.

2. Deut 34:5–6.

In the second instance, there is a *Predestinarian* position that insists emphatically on the omnipotence of God, and the implicit idea that God's ways cannot be, and do not need to be, justified to human beings. On this view, there can't really *be* a "problem" about God's justice; the only problem is our perspective on that justice. God *is* the rules. Many have tried to make sense of the Akedah in this way. God just *is* justice. God does not need to be justified to people. We see this again later in Egypt, with the Passover and Pharaoh's mysteriously hardened heart.

In the third case, and in partial response to this second point of view, the Hebrew Bible developed an almost *Karmic* position, the so-called Deuteronomic perspective, which insists that God's justice is in fact perfectly transparent and very much like our own. It involves fairly obvious rewards and punishments, clearly laid out and mandated by God in an elaborate code of laws. If you do this, then you will prosper. If you fail to do this, then you will surely suffer and die.

Max Weber, the great German sociologist of religion who lived and wrote in the early twentieth century, identified these three positions as the three most "rationally consistent" and appealing solutions to the problem of theodicy, the difficulty of explaining the existence of evil and suffering in the world, especially the suffering of the innocent. He laid it all out in two remarkably short and shattering pages.[3] What I am especially intrigued by in Weber's analysis is what I take to be its subtle conclusion: that we are inhabiting a Dualist and Predestinarian, rather than a Deuteronomic, world in the book of Genesis, a world where there are far more questions than answers, a world of mysterious if not seemingly non-existent justice. It is only later that we will witness the increasing power of human character to alter God's plans, in the book of Exodus. By the time the Torah is complete—and Deuteronomy is its fifth book—we are living in a thoroughly Karmic universe, a simpler world of just rewards and justified punishments, where God is simply responding to what God's creatures persist in doing to their own great hurt. But here, in the dim world of the ineffable biblical patriarchs—and especially in the case of Abraham, as Erich Auerbach noted—everything of importance is rendered in half-tones, frustrating shades, or shadow. We do not ever quite know where we are. Nor *who* we are. That seems important to stress, here, in these days, in North America, as we strive to give these old stories fresh legs. And wings.

3. See Gerth and Mills, *From Max Weber: Essays in Sociology*, 358–59.

Select Bibliography

Ackermann, Diane. *Cultivating Delight: A Natural History of My Garden.* New York: HarperCollins, 2001.
Armstrong, Joan. *Conditions of Love: The Philosophy of Intimacy.* New York: Penguin, 2002.
Asher, Gerald. *Vineyard Tales: Reflections on Wine.* San Francisco: Chronicle, 1996.
Auerbach, Erich. *Mimesis: The Representation of Reality in Western Literature.* Translated by Willard R. Trask. Princeton: Princeton University Press, 1953.
Baetzhold, Howard, and Joseph McCullough, editors. *The Bible According to Mark Twain.* New York: Simon and Shuster, 1995.
Bass, George. "Oldest Known Shipwreck Reveals Bronze Age Splendors." *National Geographic* 172.6 (1987) 693–732.
Boswell, John. *Christianity, Social Tolerance and Homosexuality: A History of Gay People in Europe from the Beginning of the Christian Era to the Fourteenth Century.* Chicago: University of Chicago Press, 1980.
Calasso, Roberto. *The Marriage of Cadmus and Harmony.* Translated by Tim Parks. New York: Vintage, 1993.
Capon, Robert Farrar. *Genesis: The Movie.* Grand Rapids: Eerdmans, 2003.
———. *Between Noon and Three: Romance, Law and the Outrage of Grace.* Grand Rapids: Eerdmans, 1997.
Carson, Anne. *Decreation: Poetry, Essays, Opera.* New York: Knopf, 2005.
———. *Eros the Bittersweet: An Essay.* Princeton: Princeton University Press, 1986.
———. *Glass, Irony and God.* New York: New Directions, 1995.
———. *If Not, Winter: Fragments of Sappho.* New York: Knopf, 2002.
———. *Plainwater: Essays and Poems.* New York: Vintage, 1995.
Chadwick, John. *Linear B and Related Scripts.* London: British Museum, 1986.
Coffin, David R. *The Villa in the Life of Renaissance Rome.* Princeton University Press, 1979.

Crozier, Michael, editor. "After the Garden?" Special issue, *South Atlantic Quarterly* 98.4 (Fall 1999).
Derrida, Jacques. *The Work of Mourning*. Edited by Pascale-Anne Brault and Michael Naas. Chicago: University of Chicago Press, 2001.
Diamant, Anita. *The Red Tent*. New York: Picador, 1997.
Durrell, Lawrence. *Caesar's Vast Ghost: Aspects of Provence*. With photographs by Harry Peccinotti. New York: Little, Brown, 1990.
———. *Prospero's Cell: A Guide to the Landscape and Manners of the Island of Corfu*. New York: Dutton, 1945.
———. *Reflections on a Marine Venus: A Companion to the Landscape of Rhodes*. New York: Penguin, 1952.
———. *Sicilian Carousel*. New York: Marlowe, 1976.
———. *Spirit of Place*. Edited by Alan G. Thomas. New York: Marlowe, 1969.
Elytis, Odysseas. *Maria Nephele: A Poem in Two Voices*. Translated by Athan Anagnostopoulos. Boston: Houghton Mifflin, 1981.
Feiler, Bruce. *Abraham: A Journey to the Heart of Three Faiths*. Harper Perennial, 2004.
Fox, Everett, translator. *The Five Books of Moses*. New York: Shocken, 1995.
Gerth, H. H., and C. Wright Mills, editors. *From Max Weber: Essays in Sociology*. New York: Oxford University Press, 1946.
Gesenius, William, editor. *A Hebrew and English Lexicon of the Old Testament*. Translated by Edward Robinson. New York: Oxford University Press, 1906, 1951.
Gopnik, Adam. "Voltaire's Garden." *The New Yorker*, March 7, 2005, 74–81.
Grafton, Anthony. *New Worlds, Ancient Texts: The Power of Tradition and the Shock of Discovery*. Cambridge, MA: Harvard University Press, 1992.
———, with Megan Williams. *Christianity and the Transformation of the Book*. Cambridge, MA: Harvard University Press, 2006.
Graves, Robert, and Raphael Patai, editors. *Hebrew Myths: The Book of Genesis*. New York: Crown, 1963.
Gumbrecht, Hans Ulrich. *In Praise of Athletic Beauty*. Cambridge, MA: Harvard University Press, 2006.
Halevi, Yossi Klein. *At the Entrance to the Garden of Eden: A Jew's Search for God with Christians and Muslims in the Holy Land*. New York: William Morrow, 2001.
Hamilton, Edith. *The Greek Way*. New York: Norton, 1930.
Hegel, G. W. F. *Lectures on the Philosophy of World History*. Translated by H. B. Nisbet. New York: Cambridge University Press, 1975.
———. *The Philosophy of History*. Translated by J. Sibree. Amherst, NY: Prometheus, 1991.
Heinberg, Richard. *Memories and Visions of Paradise: Exploring the Universal Myth of a Lost Golden Age*. Expanded Edition. Wheaton, IL: Quest, 1995.
Herbert, Zbigniew. *Barbarian in the Garden*. Translated by Michael March and Jaroslav Anders. New York: Harcourt Brace Jovanovich, 1985.

Hodgson, Marshall G. S. *The Venture of Islam: History and Conscience in a World Civilization*. 3 vols. Chicago: University of Chicago Press, 1974.
Hollinger, David. *Postethnic America: Beyond Multiculturalism*. 2nd ed. New York: Basic, 2000.
Impey, Oliver, and Arthur MacGregor, editors. *Garden and Grove: The Italian Renaissance Garden and the English Imagination*. London: Dent, 1986.
Jordan, Mark D. *The Invention of Sodomy in Christian Theology*. Chicago: University of Chicago Press, 1997.
Kephart, Beth. *Ghosts in the Garden: Reflections on Endings, Beginnings and the Unearthing of Self*. Novato, CA: New World Library, 2005.
Kierkegaard, Søren. *Fear and Trembling and Repetition*. Translated and edited by Howard and Edna Hong. Princeton University Press, 1953.
Kittel, Rudolf, Karl Elliger, Wilhelm Rudolph, Hans Peter Rüger, and G. E. Weil, editors. *Biblia Hebraica Stuttgartensia*. Stuttgart: Deutsche Bibelgesellschaft, 1977.
Knust, Jennifer. *Abandoned to Lust: Sexual Slander and Ancient Christianity*. New York: Columbia University Press, 2006.
Lawrence, Bruce B. *Defenders of God*. San Francisco: Harper and Row, 1989.
———, editor. *Messages to the World: The Speeches of Osama bin Laden*. New York: Verso, 2006.
Lambropoulos, Vassilis. "Building Diaspora." *Crossings: A Counter-Disciplinary Journal of Philosophical, Cultural, Historical, and Literary Studies* 1.2 (1997) 19–26.
———, editor. "Ethical Politics." Special issue: *South Atlantic Quarterly* 95.4 (1996).
———. *The Rise of Eurocentrism: Anatomy of Interpretation*. Princeton: Princeton University Press, 1994.
Leontis, Artemis. "Mediterranean Topographies Before Balkanization: On Greek Diaspora, *Emporion*, and Revolution." *Diaspora* 6.2 (1997) 179–94.
Lisle, Laurie. *Four Tenths of an Acre: Reflections on a Gardening Life*. New York: Random House, 2005.
Macauley, Rose. *The Towers of Trebizond*. New York: Farrar, Straus, and Cudahy, 1956.
Marble, Joan. *Notes From an Italian Garden*. New York: HarperCollins, 2000.
Matvejevich, Predrag. *Mediterranean: A Cultural Landscape*. Translated by Michael H. Heim. Berkeley: University of California Press, 1999.
Miller, Robert J., editor. *The Complete Gospels*. Sonoma, CA: Polebridge, 1992.
Mitchell, Henry. *The Essential Earthman*. New York: Houghton Mifflin, 1981.
Mitchell, John Hanson. *The Wildest Place on Earth: Italian Gardens and the Invention of Wilderness*. Washington, DC: Counterpoint, 2001.
Morris, Sarah P. *Daidalos and the Origins of Greek Art*. Princeton: Princeton University Press, 1992.
Morrison, Toni. *Jazz*. New York: Penguin, 1992.
———. *Love*. New York: Knopf, 2003.

Moscati, Sabatino, editor. *The Phoenicians*. New York: Abbeville, 1988.
Most, Glenn W. *Doubting Thomas*. Cambridge, MA: Harvard University Press, 2005.
Murphy, Peter, editor. "Friendship." Special issue, *South Atlantic Quarterly* 97.1 (1998).
Myer, Marvin. *Secret Gospels*. Berkeley: University of California Press, 2003.
Nasr, Seyyed Hossein. *The Heart of Islam: Enduring Values for Humanity*. San Francisco: HarperSanFrancisco, 2002.
———. *Islam: Religion, History, and Civilization*. San Francisco: HarperSanFrancisco, 2003.
Nollman, Jim. *Why We Garden: Cultivating a Sense of Place*. Boulder, CO: Sentient, 2005.
Olyan, Saul M. "'And With a Male You Shall Not Lie the Lying Down of a Woman': On the Meaning and Significance of Leviticus 18:22 and 20:13." *Journal of the History of Sexuality* 5.2 (1994) 179–206.
Otte, Jean-Pierre. *Love in the Garden*. Translated by Moishe Black and Maria Green. New York: Braziller, 2000.
Pagels, Elaine. *Adam, Eve and the Serpent*. New York: Vintage, 1988.
———. *Beyond Belief: The Secret Gospel of Thomas*. New York: Random House, 2003.
———. *The Gnostic Gospels*. New York: Vintage, 1979.
———. *The Gnostic Paul: Gnostic Exegesis of the Pauline Letters*. Harrisburg, PA: Trinity, 1975.
Percy, Walker. *Love in the Ruins*. New York: Farrar, Straus, and Giroux, 1971.
———. *Signposts in a Strange Land*. Edited by Patrick Samway. New York: Farrar, Straus, and Giroux, 1991.
Percy, William Alexander. *Lanterns on the Levee: Recollections of a Planter's Son*. Baton Rouge: Louisiana State University Press, 1941, 1973.
Peterson, Thomas V. *Ham and Japheth: The Mythic World of Whites in the Antebellum South*. Metuchen, NJ: Scarecrow, 1978.
Philo of Alexandria. *Philo in ten volumes and two supplementary volumes*. Edited by F. H. Colson, G. H. Whitaker, et al. Loeb Classical Library. Cambridge, MA: Harvard University Press, 1966–71.
Plato. *Plato in twelve volumes*. Edited by Harold North Fowler, W. R. M. Lamb, et al. Loeb Classical Library. Cambridge, MA: Harvard University Press, 1967–79.
Platt, Charles A. *Italian Gardens*. New York: Harper, 1894.
Pynchon, Thomas. *Gravity's Rainbow*. New York: Bantam, 1973.
Rahlfs, Alfred, editor. *Septuaginta*. Stuttgart: Deutsche Bibelstiftung, 1935.
Richardson, Cyril C., editor. *Early Christian Fathers*. New York: MacMillan, 1970.
Robbins, Tom. *Another Roadside Attraction*. New York: Bantam, 1971.
Robbins, Vernon K. *The Tapestry of Early Christian Discourse: Rhetoric, Society and Ideology*. New York: Routledge, 1996.

Robinson, James M. "The Discovery of the Nag Hammadi Codices." *Biblical Archaeologist* 42 (1979) 206–24.
———, editor. *The Nag Hammadi Library*. San Francisco: HarperCollins, 1977.
Ruprecht, Louis A., Jr. *Afterwords: Hellenism, Modernism and the Myth of Decadence*. Albany, NY: SUNY Press, 1996.
———. "By the Waters of Delphi: Durrell, Kazantzakis, *Achilles' Fiancée* and the Idea of Greece." Review of *Achilles' Fiancée*, by Alki Zei, translated by Gail Holst-Warhaft. *Soundings* 83.2 (2000) 331–60.
———. "God Gardened in the East, Avram Wandered West." *South Atlantic Quarterly* 98.4 (1999) 689–710.
———. "Homeric Wisdom and Heroic Friendship." *South Atlantic Quarterly* 97.1 (1998) 29–64.
———. "Righting the Self and Writing God: An Essay on Anne Carson." Forthcoming in *Thesis Eleven*, 2007.
———. "The South as Tragic Landscape." *Thesis Eleven* 85 (2006) 37–63.
———. *Symposia: Plato, the Erotic and Moral Value*. Albany, NY: SUNY Press, 1999.
———. *Tragic Posture and Tragic Vision: Against the Modern Failure of Nerve*. New York: Continuum, 1994.
———. *Was Greek Thought Religious? On the Use and Abuse of Hellenism, From Rome to Romanticism*. New York: Palgrave/MacMillan, 2002.
Sexson, Lynda. *Ordinarily Sacred*. Charlottesville, VA: University of Virginia Press, 1986.
Simon, Laura. *Dear Mr. Jefferson: Letters from a Nantucket Gardener*. New York: Dell, 1999.
Smith, Clifford L. *History of Troup County*. Atlanta: Foote and Davies, 1933.
Stern, Philip van Doren, editor. *The Life and Writings of Abraham Lincoln*. New York: Modern Library, 2000.
Strong, Sir Roy. *The Renaissance Garden*. London: Thames and Hudson, 1979.
Stout, Jeffrey. *Democracy and Tradition*. New Forum Books. Princeton: Princeton University Press, 2004.
Taylor, Charles. *Sources of the Self: The Making of the Modern Identity*. Cambridge, MA: Harvard University Press, 1989.
Trible, Phyllis. *Texts of Terror*. Philadelphia: Fortress, 1984.
Twain, Mark. *Huckleberry Finn* [1885]. Chicago: Scott, Foresman, c1951.
———. *The Innocents Abroad* [1869]. New York: Airmont, 1967.
———. *Letters from the Earth*. Edited by Bernard DeVoto. New York: HarperCollins, 1962.
Ussher, James. *The Annals of the World*. London: Tyler, Crook and Bedell, 1685.
La Villa in Italia: Una Tradizione di Civilita. Bolis Edizione, 2002.
Wasserstein, Abraham, and David J. Wasserstein. *The Legend of the Septuagunt: From Classical Antiquity to Today*. New York: Cambridge University Press, 2006.

Watts, Edward J. *City and School in Late Antique Athens and Alexandria*. Berkeley: University of California Press, 2006.
Wharton, Edith. *Italian Villas and Their Gardens*. New York: Century, 1904.
Wiesel, Elie. *Messengers of God: Biblical Portraits and Legends*. Translated by Marion Wiesel. New York: Summit, 1976.
Wild, Anthony. *The East India Company: Trade and Conquest From 1600*. New York: Lyons of HarperCollins, 1999.
Winkler, Carol K. *In the Name of Terrorism: Presidents on Political Violence in the Post-World War II Era*. Albany, NY: SUNY Press, 2006.
Wise, Michael, Martin Abegg Jr., and Edward Cook, editors. *The Dead Sea Scrolls*. San Francisco: HarperSanFrancisco, 1996.
Wright, W. C., editor. *The Works of the Emperor Julian in 3 Volumes*. Loeb Classical Library. Cambridge, MA: Harvard University Press.

www.ingramcontent.com/pod-product-compliance
Lightning Source LLC
Chambersburg PA
CBHW030111170426
43198CB00009B/582